Adobe®
Photoshop®
by Design

Hayden
Books

Photoshop by Design

Photoshop Bikkuri Character Design.
Copyright ©1998 MdN Corporation All rights reserved. Original edition published in Japan by MdN Corporation. English Language edition copyright ©1999 Macmillan Computer Publishing USA. This book is published and distributed in English by Hayden Books, a Division of Macmillan Computer Publishing, USA.

All rights reserved. No part of this book shall be reproduced, stored in a retrieval system, or transmitted by any means, electronic, mechanical, photocopying recording or otherwise without written permission from Macmillan Computer Publishing and/or MdN Corporation. No patent liability is assumed with respect to the use of the information contained herein. Although every precaution has been taken in the preparation of this book, the publisher and authors assume no responsibility for errors or omissions. Neither is any liability assumed for damage resulting from the use of the information contained herein.

International Standard Book Number: 0-7897-2084-1
Library of Congress Catalog Card Number: 99-65635

Printed in the United States
First Printing of English Edition: August 1999
Trademarks

Apple, AppleScript, Mac, Macintosh and Power Macintosh are registered trademarks of Apple Computer, Inc. Microsoft and Windows are registered trademarks and Windows NT is a trademark of Microsoft Corporation in the United States and other countries. Adobe, Illustrator, Photoshop and Acrobat are trademarks of Adobe Systems Incorporated. All other brand names, product names, trademarks and registered trademarks belong to the respective holders.

Character Production/Design
Special Thanks to:
Hi! Seisaku-shitsu Ltd. (1-1, 1-2, 1-3, 1-7, 1-9) Kazuhiko Wakita (1-4, 1-5, 1-8, 1-10, 1-12)
Yuri Hanayama(1-6,1-11,2-1,2-2,2-5,2-6,3-1,3-2)Yoko Ogre(2-3,2-4,3-3,3-4,3-5,3-6)

Japanese edition produced by: MdN Book Division
Editor: Mari Funaki
Design/Production: Mamoru Jun'i / Natsuko Inaba (Hi! Seisaku-shitsu Ltd.)

Image Supplier: Data Craft Co. Ltd.

Fonts: Brian J. Bonislawsky, Astigmatic One Eye Foundry CD Production: DDN Co. Ltd.
English Translation by DNA Media Services Inc.

Contents

Chapter 2 Photo Editing **131**

To the Reader

Thank you for purchasing Adobe Photoshop by Design. This book goes beyond any previous Photoshop guide to provide specific explanations of the procedures for generating a wide range of characters and illustrations. If you follow the clearly-explained sequences, you should be able to complete the characters exactly as shown. It is not a book you need to read from cover-to-cover, but something you can pick up and start anywhere. Feel free to start with any character that catches your attention. For assistance with program commands, see the Photoshop Fundamentals section starting on p 13.

■

This book provides instructions for users of both the Macintosh and Windows platforms. Where instructions are different for the two, Macintosh instructions are written in lowercase letters and Windows instructions are written in uppercase letters encased in brackets.

■

The supplementary CD-ROM is a hybrid disk containing both the Macintosh and Windows versions of the software and data. Please see the Supplementary CD-ROM section on p 11 for more information.

INTRODUCTION

Before you dive in and start designing cute characters, please take a few moments to read through this chapter. It explains the book's basic assumptions and approach, the CD-ROM contents and the fundamentals of using Photoshop. Glance through this summary first to better understand the procedures required throughout the production process. This will make your work proceed more smoothly. If you get stuck implementing a step later in the book, simply return to this chapter to find the answers.

About this Book

RECOMMENDED SYSTEM CONFIGURATION

To use Photoshop 5.0, Adobe recommends 32 MB RAM on Power Macintosh and systems running Windows 95 or Windows NT. Although the minimum requirement for a Macintosh with a 68030 or higher processor is 24 MB, more memory is recommended. Refer to the documentation in the software package for detailed system requirements for Photoshop 5.0.

ADOBE PHOTOSHOP 5.0

Since all illustrations in this Book were created with Adobe Photoshop 5.0, you are advised to use version 5.0 if at all possible. Earlier versions can produce different results even with the instructions provided in this Book. All illustrations in this book can be created with Photoshop 4.0, but the procedures will be different because some functions have changed in version 5.0. Please check Adobe's web site, (http://www.adobe.com/), which is frequently updated, to obtain the latest information on Adobe products, user groups, software tutorials and version upgrades.

IMAGE FILE SETTINGS

All images in this book were created in the RGB mode at a resolution of either 72 or 300 pixels/inch (ppi). Although you can use the color mode of your preference, please note that some of the suggested procedures may have to be adapted. Please also note that the reproduced color range changes with the color mode. There may be significant differences between the colors in RGB mode and CMYK mode, for example, even with the same color values when images are viewed on screen and when viewed in print.

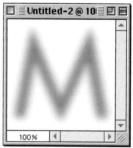

150 x 150 pixels

Note: Many of the examples were created with filters that can only be used in the RGB mode. See the *Adobe Photoshop User Guide* for details on differences in the color modes.

300 x 300 pixels

In addition to being RGB mode images, the examples in this book were created at an image resolution of 72 or 300 ppi. In each case, the image size is specified in pixel dimensions. To accurately reproduce the images shown in this manual, the image files should be created with the same color modes and resolutions (pixel dimensions). You shouldn't have problems creating exact copies if you use the specified dimensions. However, changing them will alter the effects of filters and commands. For example, a Gaussian blur of 6 pixels will reduce more detail on an image of 150 x 150 pixels than on one of 300 x 300 pixels (see the illustration of the eMi). If you decide to change the specified pixel dimensions, compare your image to that shown to the right of each procedure and make appropriate adjustments to achieve the closest results.

HOW PROCEDURES ARE DESCRIBED

Menu Commands

The following notation is used to describe the selection of commands in this book.

Select Filter > Blur > Gaussian Blur

This example indicates the procedures for applying the Gaussian Blur filter. First, click Filter on the menu bar at the top of the screen and drag the cursor down to Blur on the pull-down menu. When Blur is highlighted, a submenu opens to the right. Drag the cursor down to Gaussian Blur in the submenu and release the mouse (Figure 1). A dialog box appears for you to specify parameters. Some commands do not require dialog boxes but are executed directly. Settings and values required to create each example are listed in the dialog box (Figure 2). Click OK to execute the command (Figure 3).

Figure 1

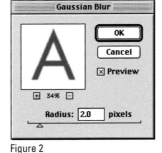

Figure 2

Figure 3

Specifying Numeric Values and Options

The numeric values and options described in the procedures are those required to reproduce the given example. Since the optimal settings may differ for each graphic, use the suggested settings as guidelines only. Photoshop novices will find it useful to try the suggested settings at first.

> ## TIPS
> This book also includes TIPS, which contain information supplementary to the basic procedures in each chapter.

The simple example of light and shadows (the 10:00 and 4:00 rule) is quoted several times in this publication. This technique makes an object appear to pop out of the screen. Recently dubbed '2.5D' or 'pseudo-3D', it is a classic technique for representing volume, perspective and reality. A clock face is used here to explain the process in simple terms. To produce a sphere, as below, use a white airbrush to highlight a circle around the 10 o'clock area. Next, use a black airbrush to apply a shadow around the 4 o'clock position. This combination of highlighting and shadowing creates the illusion of a three-dimensional sphere.

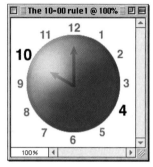

Highlight the 10:00 position

Shadow the 4:00 position

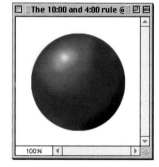

Finished pseudo-3D sphere

Supplementary CD-ROM

The supplementary CD-ROM contains finished illustrations, materials for creating illustrations, template files and other items related to the illustrations in this book.

Folder for Windows

The CD-ROM can be used on either the Macintosh or Windows (Windows 95 or later versions only) platform.

Folder for Macintosh

Chapters 2 and 3 introduce high-resolution illustrations that may take a long time to process or may incur other problems, such as insufficient memory to open sample materials, on systems with limited memory. If the high-resolution materials pose a problem, low-resolution samples have also been provided. File names ending with [_150] are 150 dpi, or low-resolution data, while those ending with [_300] are 300 dpi, or high-resolution data.

Unless otherwise noted, the data on the supplementary CD-ROM is for use with the lessons in this book or for reference purposes only. The copyright to the data belongs to the respective producers and MdN Corporation. You are prohibited from transferring, selling or using the data for profit without permission.

The following two materials contained in the CD-ROM are recorded from the clip art collection and clip art dictionary series of Data Craft Inc., whose assistance we gratefully acknowledge.

2-05 folder   teatime.psd
(Clip Art Dictionary Vol. 22   Food/Cuisine Image Collection SW074)
2-06 folder   fruits.psd
(Clip Art Dictionary Vol. 22   Food/Cuisine Image Collection SW051)

These images are for use solely as materials for lessons in this book. You must purchase a commercial version of the data directly from the producer to use it for any other purpose, whether for profit or not.

Contact Data Craft Inc. at:
SE Sankyo Building
1-2 Nishi 1-Chome, 7 Jo, Kita-ku
Sapporo, Japan 060-0807
Telephone: +81 (011) 707-8335

SAMPLE DATA

The Sample Data folder on the supplementary CD-ROM contains finished image data created for this book as well as textures and photographs used in creating the graphics. All image data can be opened with Photoshop 4.0 or 5.0. Gradient files, fonts and action files are also supplied. These materials are organized for use with each example. To find the data, check the folder bearing the same number as the example.

SOFTWARE

The Software folder on the supplementary CD-ROM contains demo versions of Adobe Photoshop 5.0 and Adobe Illustrator 8.0. Please read the Read Me files to learn how to install or use the software. Note that the demo version of Photoshop can't execute all the techniques in this book and cannot save files.

TEMPLATES

The templates of products photographed for this book are stored in EPS files. This data was created using Adobe Illustrator 7.0 and features characters presented in this Photoshop manual. Users of Adobe Illustrator 7.0 can also use this data and replace the characters with their own original works for printout.

Note: If a system error is caused by opening a template file on a Macintosh, open the 'Sharing' control panel and turn off 'File Sharing' before trying to open a template again.

Photoshop Fundamentals

This chapter summarizes the basic graphic techniques and Photoshop procedures required by beginners. The chapter is based on the following two assumptions: that either Photoshop 5.0 or Photoshop tools (toolbox) will be used to process graphics and that each palette must always be open. To open a palette, select its name from the Window menu. Refer to the Photoshop User Guide if you are using a version prior to Photoshop 5.0. Please also note that the Layer function cannot be used with Version 2.5 or earlier versions. Macintosh keys for commands or functions are presented first in lower case letters and the corresponding Windows keys are written in upper case and enclosed in parentheses ().

PHOTOSHOP TOOLBOX

Individuals not familiar with the Photoshop toolbox will find that a little practice is all that is required to become acquainted with each tool's features. All the Photoshop 4.0 and 5.0 tools are shown below for novice users. Experienced users will find these diagrams useful as a refresher.

PHOTOSHOP 4.0 TOOLBOX

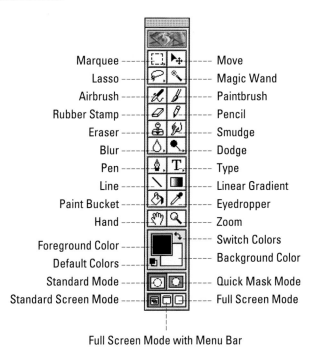

Marquee ----- Move
Lasso ----- Magic Wand
Airbrush ----- Paintbrush
Rubber Stamp ----- Pencil
Eraser ----- Smudge
Blur ----- Dodge
Pen ----- Type
Line ----- Linear Gradient
Paint Bucket ----- Eyedropper
Hand ----- Zoom
Foreground Color ----- Switch Colors
Default Colors ----- Background Color
Standard Mode ----- Quick Mask Mode
Standard Screen Mode ----- Full Screen Mode

Full Screen Mode with Menu Bar

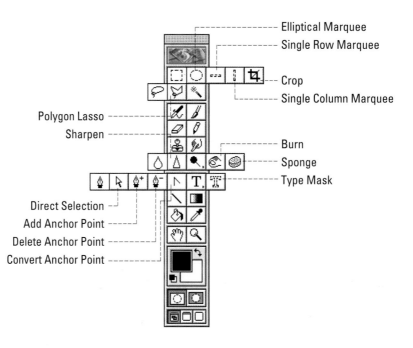

Elliptical Marquee
Single Row Marquee
Crop
Single Column Marquee

Polygon Lasso
Sharpen

Burn
Sponge
Type Mask

Direct Selection
Add Anchor Point
Delete Anchor Point
Convert Anchor Point

PHOTOSHOP 5.0 TOOLBOX

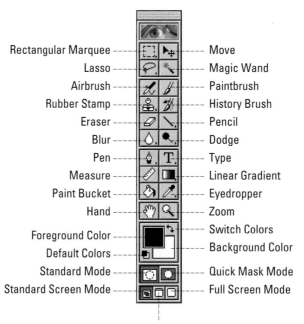

Rectangular Marquee ----- Move
Lasso ----- Magic Wand
Airbrush ----- Paintbrush
Rubber Stamp ----- History Brush
Eraser ----- Pencil
Blur ----- Dodge
Pen ----- Type
Measure ----- Linear Gradient
Paint Bucket ----- Eyedropper
Hand ----- Zoom

Foreground Color ----- Switch Colors
Default Colors ----- Background Color
Standard Mode ----- Quick Mask Mode
Standard Screen Mode ----- Full Screen Mode

Full Screen Mode with Menu Bar

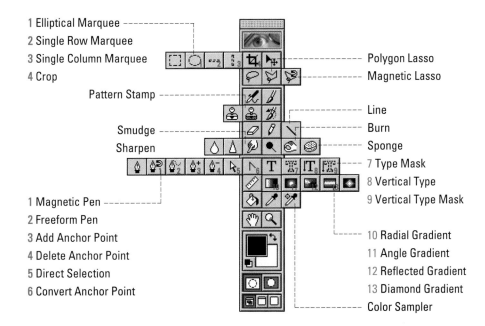

1 Elliptical Marquee
2 Single Row Marquee
3 Single Column Marquee
4 Crop

Pattern Stamp

Smudge
Sharpen

Polygon Lasso
Magnetic Lasso

Line
Burn
Sponge
7 Type Mask
8 Vertical Type
9 Vertical Type Mask

1 Magnetic Pen
2 Freeform Pen
3 Add Anchor Point
4 Delete Anchor Point
5 Direct Selection
6 Convert Anchor Point

10 Radial Gradient
11 Angle Gradient
12 Reflected Gradient
13 Diamond Gradient
Color Sampler

IMAGES AND RESOLUTION

It is essential to clarify the purpose of an image being created at the outset. If the image is to be displayed in a multimedia presentation or on a web page, then a monitor resolution of 72 dpi is appropriate. In this case, the final image is what you see on your monitor. In contrast, print images require completely different treatment. They usually require an image resolution of 300 dpi. An image file created at 50 x 50 pixels would appear as a 1/2 x 1/2 inch image on the monitor, but would print as a 1/6 x 1/6 inch image. Fine details, especially areas processed with the Add Noise filter, would not reproduce adequately. You can preserve image detail by increasing the pixel dimensions (higher resolution) of the final image, although raising the resolution too high is not recommended. To preserve as much detail as possible, the Nearest Neighbor interpolation method is best for increasing resolution. This method avoids anti-aliasing when the resolution is raised. The printed image will reproduce correctly as long as the enlargement is kept below 300% of the original size, although it will appear pixelated on the monitor. See page p18 for the procedures for increasing pixel dimensions.

OPTIONS PALETTE

Select Window > Show Options to display the Options palette corresponding to the selected tool. Alternatively, you can display these options by double-clicking the required tool in the toolbox. Use this palette to specify the blending mode, pressure or other parameters of the applicable tool. In this book, the phrase specify 'set _ to _' or similar wording refers to the Options palette for a selected tool unless another palette is identified.

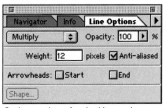

Options palette for the Line tool

Creating a New File

To create a new file or document, select File > New. Input a name for the file and other settings in the New dialog box. Refer to How Procedures Are Described on p 9 for an explanation of the command notation in this book

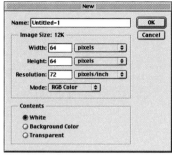

Shortcut   command (Ctrl) + N

New Dialog Box

Adding Horizontal/Vertical Guides

Guide lines can be displayed over the top of a Photoshop file. Select View > Show Rulers to display rulers along the top and left side of the active window. Then choose View > Show Guides.

Shortcut   Show or Hide Rulers: command (Ctrl) + R
Show or Hide Guides: command (Ctrl) + ;

Active window with displayed guides

You can add a guide with any tool by dragging out from a ruler. To move a guide, select the Move tool and drag the guide. If a tool other than the Move tool is in use, hold down the command (Ctrl) key as you drag. To remove a guide, drag it back to the respective ruler.

Show Guides command

TIPS

You can make a guide snap to the ruler increments by holding down the shift (Shift) key while dragging the guide. A horizontal guide can also be changed to a vertical guide, or vice versa, by holding down the option (Alt) key while dragging it.

Setting Guide and Grid Preferences

The guide color, grid spacing and other attributes can be adjusted. To set guide and grid preferences, select File > Preferences > Guides & Grid. Specify the attributes in the Preferences dialog box, which can also be used to adjust other settings.

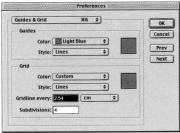

Preferences dialog box

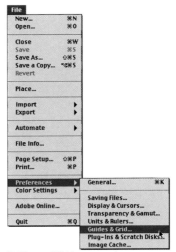

Guides and Grid command

Ruler Units

Select View > Show Rulers and View > Show Grid to have the rulers and grid displayed on the screen. Grid units are specified using File > Preferences > Guides & Grid as explained previously. Ruler units are specified using File > Preferences > Units & Rulers. In this book, the ruler units are pixels unless otherwise specified.

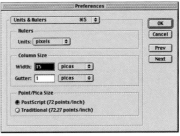

Preferences dialog box

Changing the Painting Cursor

To change the painting cursors to the selected brush size, choose File > Preferences > Screen Display/Cursor. In the Preferences dialog box, click Brush Size in the Painting Cursors section. This option is useful to ascertain brush sizes while working on a subject. Return the setting to Standard when the work is finished.

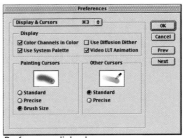

Preferences dialog box

Duplicating Images

To duplicate an active image, select Image > Duplicate. Click Merged Layers Only in the Duplicate Image dialog box to duplicate the image without layers.

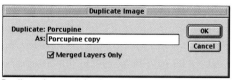

Duplicate Image dialog box

Increasing Pixel Dimensions

If an image is too small when output or the edges are too rough because of inadequate resolution, the pixel dimensions (file size) should be increased. To change the pixel dimensions, select Image > Image Size. Click Resample Image at the bottom of the Image Size dialog box and increase the Width and Height values in the Pixel Dimensions section.

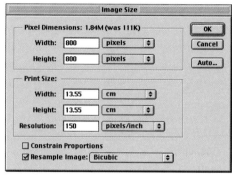

Image Size dialog box

Using Drag and Drop

You can drag and drop images from one file to another, which will copy it to the second file. Use the Move tool or hold down the command (Ctrl) key with any other selected tool. The drag-and-drop method eliminates the need to copy an image onto the clipboard before pasting it into the work area. You can copy an image to the center of a file by holding down the shift (Shift) key while dragging it. This technique is effective for dragging an entire image or for dragging a layer onto the Layers palette. Two images of the same size can be overlapped precisely with this technique.

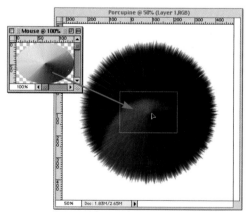

Drag and drop an image onto another file

Changing Color Modes

Photoshop supports a number of color modes, including RGB, CMYK and Grayscale. To change the color mode, choose Image > Mode, and select a mode from the submenu. The current color mode is indicated by a check mark. For example, to convert from RGB to CMYK mode, select Image > Mode > CMYK Color. The next time this menu is displayed, the check mark previously beside RGB Color will now be beside CMYK Color, the current mode.

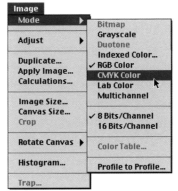

Mode menu

TIPS

Changing the color mode of an image alters the range of colors available for its reproduction. Photoshop prints all color output, with a few exceptions, in CMYK mode regardless of the color mode selected for the Photoshop file. The output colors may change as a result of this automatic conversion. For example, colors that appear as bright green on the monitor may appear as dark brown in the printout. If you wish to output in a mode other than CMYK, you must first convert it to CYMK in Photoshop to verify how the colors change before converting it back and printing it.

Inputting Text

Before inputting text with the Type tool, ensure that the right foreground color is selected for the text. Characters input with the Text tool are automatically added as a new layer. Select the Type tool and click anywhere within the image. Enter the text into the large box at the bottom of the Type Tool dialog box, then specify the options above this box as required. Select the Anti-Aliased option unless otherwise directed.

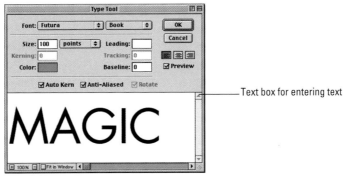

Text box for entering text

Type Tool dialog box

Loading Brush Files

In Photoshop, brush shapes can be added to the default brushes. To load a brush file, select Load Brushes from the Brushes palette menu. A brush file can be added to the default brushes, or a default brush can be saved in a new brush file. Brush files are usually supplied with Photoshop.

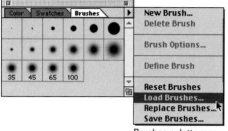

Brushes palette menu

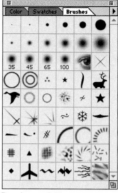

Brushes palette

Creating New Brushes

In this book, you will use brushes of various sizes not included in the default brushes. To create a new brush, select New Brush from the Brushes palette menu. To create a hard brush, use the settings shown in the New Brush dialog box to the right. Set the brush size by specifying its diameter. For a soft brush, set the Hardness option to 0%.

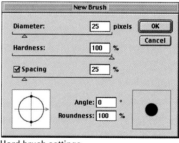

Hard brush settings

Using Filters

Various filters are available in Photoshop for applying special effects to images. Numerous plug-in filters supported by Photoshop have also been released by third parties. To use a filter, select the desired submenu and command from the Filter menu. A dialog box will appear for some filters, allowing you to fine-tune the parameters and preview the affected portion of the image.

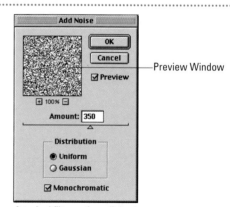

A typical filter options dialog box

Defining the Original Sampling Point for the Rubber Stamp Tool

The Rubber Stamp tool copies the portions of an image over which it is passed. To define the original sampling point, select the Rubber Stamp tool, hold the option key and click (Alt-click) on a point in the image. Then click on a different point in the image with the Rubber Stamp tool to paint a copy of the sampled area to the new area. The Rubber Stamp tool brush shape and opacity settings can be freely changed.

Defining Patterns

A portion of an image can be defined as a pattern that can be repeated as tiles to fill a selection. To define the pattern, choose Select > All, or use the Rectangular Marquee tool to select an area, and select Edit > Define Pattern.

Filling a Selection with Patterns

Once you have defined a pattern, press shift + delete (Shift + Backspace) to display the Fill dialog box. Or, select Edit > Fill. Set the Contents section to Pattern to fill the selection with the defined pattern.

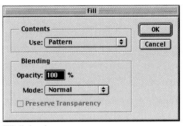

Fill dialog box

Switching Blending Modes

The Blending mode is often used as an alternative way to view layers, to fade the effect of a filter while painting with the foreground color, or to apply other effects. You can use it to determine the result color when a new blend color is applied to the original (base) color (the blend color is the foreground color belonging to the upper layer or the image after a filter has been applied. The base color is the background color, or the color belonging to the image over which you are painting, a lower layer, or the image before a filter was applied). It is relatively easy to understand the effects of some blending modes, such as Lighten, which compares the base color to the blend color and selects the lighter of the two as the result color. For the others, however, you are better off experimenting to get a feel for the effects rather than attempting to memorize the method by which colors are added or subtracted in each mode. In most instances the opacity option is chosen simultaneously with the blending mode, providing numerous variations for experimentation.

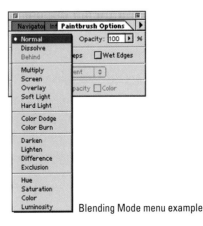

Blending Mode menu example

Saving Files

To save a file for the first time, or to save a file in its current format after changes have been made, select File > Save. To save as a different file, select File > Save As. The Save dialog box appears if a file is being saved for the first time or saved under a different name. Input (or change) the file name and choose the file format. The formats available will vary according to the image type, the contents being saved in the file, the purpose of the file and other variables. For further details, see the Photoshop User Guide or a 'how-to' book.

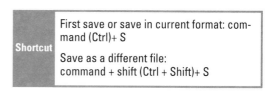

Shortcut

First save or save in current format: command (Ctrl)+ S

Save as a different file:
command + shift (Ctrl + Shift)+ S

Dialog box for saving files

Saving Copies of a File

To save a copy of the original file while editing, select File > Save a Copy. Specify the file name and the file format in the Save Copy dialog box (shown to the right). This command saves a copy of a file and displays the required layers without destroying or writing over the data of the original file. It is especially useful for saving files for use in animation sequences.

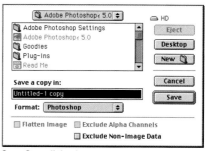

Save Copy dialog box

FOREGROUND COLOR AND BACKGROUND COLOR

The foreground and background colors can be switched from one to the other by clicking on the Switch Colors icon in the toolbox.

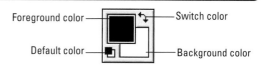

Foreground color — Switch color

Default color — Background color

Changing the Foreground or Background Color

To change the foreground or background color, click on either icon in the toolbox. In the Color Picker dialog box, select a color by positioning and clicking the cursor (which appears as a ring) within the spectrum, or by specifying a value for each component of the RGB, CMYK or other color model.

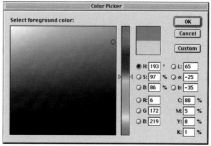

Color Picker dialog box

Resetting the Default Foreground and Background Colors

Click on the Default Colors icon in the toolbox to reset the default colors (black foreground, white background).

Shortcut D key

(If you are working with a layer mask or alpha channel, the foreground will reset to white and the background to

Filling Selections with Foreground or Background Colors

Start by selecting the desired background color and foreground fill color. Then select Edit > Fill. In the Fill dialog box, select a color and specify the opacity and blending mode.

Shortcut Press shift + delete (Shift + Backspace) to display the Fill dialog box

Alternatively, you can fill the selection with the foreground color when the selection is active by pressing option + delete (Alt + Backspace). To fill the selection with the background color when the background layer is active, press delete (Backspace), or press command + delete (Ctrl + Backspace) when you are working on a layer on which Preserve Transparency is not selected.

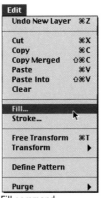

Fill command

TIPS

If a layer has the Preserve Transparency option checked, a selection containing a transparent area (a portion containing no pixels) cannot be filled. To fill this area, first switch off Preserve Transparency, and then fill it. See 'Preserving a Layer's Transparency' on p 34.

Fill dialog box

SELECTION AREAS AND MASKS

Deselecting a Selection

To deselect a selection, choose Select > None. Or, choose any selection tool other than the Magic Wand tool and click outside the selected area. The dotted border surrounding the selected area will extinguish and cancel the selection.

Shortcut command (Ctrl) + D key

Deselect Selection command

Saving a Selection

To store a selection shape, choose Select > Save Selection. The Save Selection dialog box will appear, allowing you to choose options as required.

Shortcut

Click the Save Selection icon on the Channels palette. See p 26 for an explanation of the Channels palette.

You can also display the Load Selection dialog box by holding down the option (Alt) key in the Channels palette while dragging the channel onto the Load Selection icon.

Save Selection command

Save Selection dialog box

Loading a Selection

To load a selection, choose Select > Load Selection. Specify the document to be loaded and the channel in the Load Selection dialog box. The selection can be added to or subtracted from an existing selection. A selection can be loaded from a layer as well as a channel. See 'Loading a Layer as a Selection' on p 29.

Load Selection command

Shortcut

Hold down the command (Ctrl) key in the Channels palette and click on the channel containing the selection to be loaded. See p 26 for an explanation of the Channels palette.

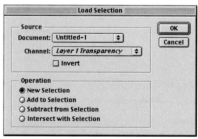

Load Selection dialog box

Showing and Hiding the Selection Border

When working with subtle highlights and shadows, the results can be more easily reviewed by temporarily hiding the broken lines enclosing the selection. To hide the selection border, choose View > Hide Edges. When Hide Edges is chosen, the View Menu changes it to Show Edges, allowing you to select this item to redisplay the selection border.

Shortcut	command (Ctrl)+ H key

Hide Edges command

Entering and Leaving the Quick Mask Mode

A mask is used to isolate and protect areas of an image being edited. If only part of an image is selected, tools and filters will affect only the selected area. In this case, the area that is not selected is masked or protected from editing. Aside from this selection method, Photoshop provides sophisticated masking functions, such as Alpha channels (p 26), Layer Masks (p 31) and the Quick Mask mode. The Quick Mask mode is probably the quickest and easiest mask function to manipulate. Any Photoshop tool and function can be used with the Quick Mask mode, which allows only the areas outside the mask to be edited. The masked portion is unaffected. After masking an area and returning to Standard mode, the unmasked area becomes the new selection. The mask is lost upon leaving the Quick Mask mode, but it is convenient to use if there is no need to retain the mask. To retain a mask, it must be created and stored as an alpha channel. To switch to the Quick Mask mode, click on the Quick Mask mode icon in the toolbox. To leave this mode, click on the Standard mode icon.

Shortcut	Use the Q key to switch between Quick Mask mode and Standard mode.

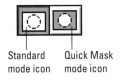

Standard mode icon   Quick Mask mode icon

An image in Quick Mask mode. The area covered in red is masked (protected). Returning to Standard mode will result in only the dog is face being selected and editable.

In addition to the default color channels that contain the color information of an image, Photoshop features alpha channels for creating and storing masks.

A channel itself is edited in the image window, but commands such as switching, adding, and deleting channels are executed with the Channels palette.

Channels palette

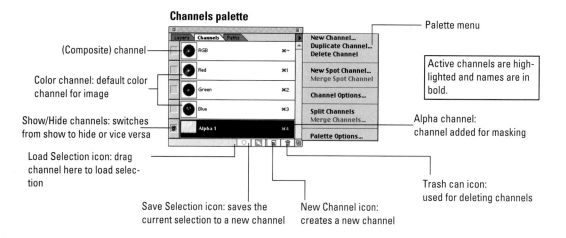

(Composite) channel

Color channel: default color channel for image

Show/Hide channels: switches from show to hide or vice versa

Load Selection icon: drag channel here to load selection

Save Selection icon: saves the current selection to a new channel

New Channel icon: creates a new channel

Palette menu

Active channels are highlighted and names are in bold.

Alpha channel: channel added for masking

Trash can icon: used for deleting channels

Creating New Channels

To create a new channel, select New Channel from the Channels palette menu. Type a name for the channel and specify the color swatch and other options on the New Channel dialog box. The default Photoshop settings are always used for new channels in the examples in this book unless otherwise stipulated. The default values are shown to the right.

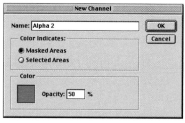

Default settings for the Channel Settings dialog box

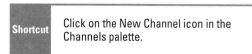

| Shortcut | Click on the New Channel icon in the Channels palette. |

Selecting Channels

Both color and alpha channels can be edited. To edit or alter a channel, the channel must be active (selected). To select a channel, click the channel name on the Channels palette. Active channels are highlighted and the names are bolded.

Duplicating Channels

To duplicate a channel, select it on the Channels palette, then choose Duplicate Channel from the palette menu. Type a name for the duplicate channel and specify other options in the Duplicate Channel dialog box.

Duplicate Channel dialog box

<table>
<tr><td>Shortcut</td><td>Drag the channel to be duplicated onto the new channel icon in the Channels palette.</td></tr>
</table>

Deleting Channels

To delete a channel, select it on the Channels palette, then choose Delete Channel from the palette menu.

Drag the channel to the trash can.

<table>
<tr><td>Shortcut</td><td>Drag the channel onto the trash can icon on the Channels palette. This procedure is similar to dragging a document from the desktop onto the trash can.</td></tr>
</table>

Returning to the Composite Channel

A composite channel displays the color information of all the channels. It is displayed on the Channels palette as 'command symbol (Ctrl) + ~' after its name. Select this channel to return to the composite channel. All color channels are automatically active if the composite channel is active. For example, in the RGB mode, each component channel, namely the R (red), G (green) and B (blue) channels, will be active.

Palette with active composite channel.

<table>
<tr><td>Shortcut</td><td>command (Ctrl) + ~ key</td></tr>
</table>

Layers are like transparent film that can be successively overlaid onto a background image. They enable an image file to be created in stages. An area of an image can be edited as an independent object on one layer, and editing one layer will not affect the others. The stacking order can be freely changed.

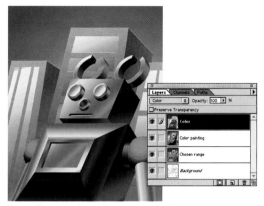

Image file comprised of layers and the Layers palette

Layers palette

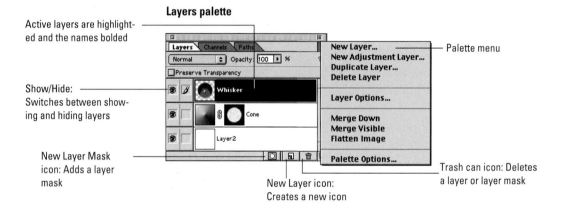

Active layers are highlighted and the names bolded

Show/Hide: Switches between showing and hiding layers

New Layer Mask icon: Adds a layer mask

Palette menu

New Layer icon: Creates a new icon

Trash can icon: Deletes a layer or layer mask

Creating New Layers

To create a new layer, select New Layer from the Layers palette menu; or choose Layer > New Layer. Name it and specify its options in the New Layer dialog box.

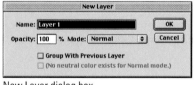

New Layer dialog box

Shortcut	Click on the New Layer icon in the Layers palette. Option-click (Alt-click) the icon to display the New Layer dialog box.

Active Layers

To edit and make changes to a layer, the layer must be active (selected). To select a layer, click the layer on the Layers palette. The active layer is highlighted and its name bolded.

Showing or Hiding Layers

To show the contents of a layer, click the left-most column on the Layers palette. An eye icon indicates the layer is visible. The layer is hidden if the eye icon is not visible.

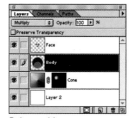

Palette with
the Body layer visible

Palette with
the Body layer hidden

Changing the Stacking Order of Layers

To bring a layer forward or send it backward, select it on the Layers palette and drag it up or down to the desired position in the list. The line between two layers is highlighted in black while a layer is being dragged, making it easy to determine its current position. The stacking order of the moved layer will change and the layer name will also shift in the Layers palette.

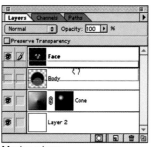

Moving a layer

Loading a Layer as a Selection Area

You can load the transparent area of a layer as a selection mask (if inverted, the non-transparent areas become selected). Choose Select > Load Selection, then select the 'Transparent area of the layer' in the Channel section of the Load Selection dialog box.

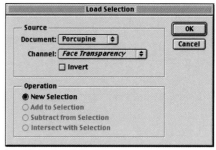

Load Selection dialog box

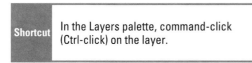

Shortcut In the Layers palette, command-click (Ctrl-click) on the layer.

Creating Layer 0

Blending modes or opacity options are not available on the background layer. To apply them to the data on the background layer, you must first convert it to Layer 0. Double-click on the Background layer in the Layers palette, then press the return (Enter) key or click OK in the dialog box. Layer 0 will be automatically created. The data on this layer is separated from the background (the Background layer is eliminated), and blending modes and opacity options can be applied.

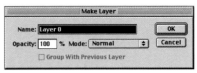

Create Layer dialog box

Creating a New (Background) Layer

This procedure is valid only if a background layer does not already exist. Select Layer > New Layer > Background to create a new background.

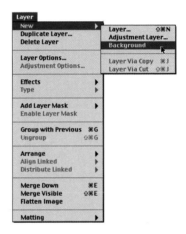

Deleting Layers

To delete a layer, select it on the Layers palette and drag it onto the trash can icon at the bottom right of the palette. This is similar in concept to dragging an icon onto the trash can in Windows 95 or the Mac OS Finder. A layer can also be deleted by selecting it and choosing Delete Layer from the Layers palette menu or Layers menu.

Deleting layer using the Layers palette

Creating an Adjustment Layer

The adjustment layer function can be used to make color and tonal adjustments to all underlying layers. Multiple layers can be corrected with a single adjustment layer without resorting to separate adjustments for each. As with image layers, an adjustment layer can be rearranged, deleted, hidden or duplicated. To create an adjustment layer, select Layer > New > Adjustment Layer; or select New Adjustment Layer from the Layers palette menu. To adjust specific layers only, turn on 'Group with Previous Layer' in the dialog box. To adjust the color or tone of a selected area, select the area before creating the adjustment layer. Choose the desired type of adjustment layer in the New Adjustment Layer dialog box. The adjustments used most often in this book are Level Correction and Hue/Saturation. The blending mode for the adjustment layer can also be changed in this dialog box.

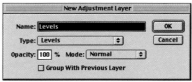

New Adjustment Layer dialog box

Adjustment Type pop-up menu

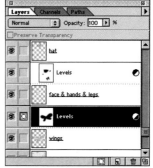

Layers palette with active adjustment layer

| Shortcut | Command-click (Ctrl-click) on the New Layer icon on the Layers palette. |

Creating a Layer Mask

A layer mask is a mask applied only to a selected layer. It is used to hide, or mask, sections of the image on the layer. The hidden or masked areas of a layer are transparent to the layer below. Like alpha channels, the layer mask is also displayed in grayscale mode. Areas painted black indicate portions of the image hidden on the selected layer and revealed on the layer below, and areas painted white indicate portions revealed on the selected layer. However, the layer mask thumbnail on the Layers palette is the only means by which the layer mask can be viewed as a Grayscale image. To create a layer mask, select Layer > Add Layer Mask > Reveal All, or Layer > Add Layer Mask > Hide All. The Reveal All command creates a mask that reveals the entire layer (white mask). The Hide All command creates a mask that hides the entire layer

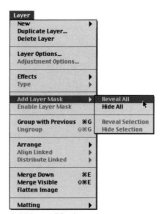

Add Layer Mask menu

(black mask). The Paintbrush tool or other tools can be used to edit a layer mask. Pre-selected (or unselected) portions of the image can also be masked. You can also create a mask by clicking the New Layer Mask icon on the Layers palette. Dragging the layer mask icon to the trash can on the Layers palette deletes the mask, which can be applied before it is deleted (click Discard or Apply). In the diagram to the right, the border of the thumbnail is highlighted to indicate that the layer mask has been selected.

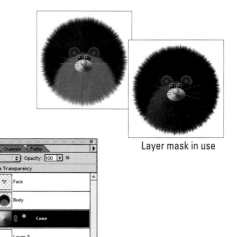

Layer mask in use

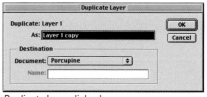

Layers Palette with a layer mask in use

Duplicating Layers

To duplicate a layer, select it on the Layers palette, then choose Duplicate Layer from the palette menu. Type a name for the duplicate layer and select options in the Duplicate Layer dialog box.

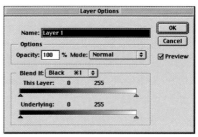

Duplicate Layer dialog box

Shortcut	On the Layers palette, click on the layer and drag it to the New Layer icon.

Renaming Layers

To rename a layer, double click on its name on the Layers palette and type a new name in the Layer Options dialog box.

Layer Options dialog box

Merging a Layer with the Layer Below

To merge a layer with the layer below it, select the upper layer and choose Layer > Merge Down. Ensure that the lower layer is visible before performing this step.

Shortcut	command (Ctrl) + E key

Merge Down command

Merging All Visible Layers

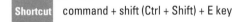

To merge all the visible layers, select Layer > Merge Visible. Ensure that all layers to be merged are visible before performing this step.

Shortcut	command + shift (Ctrl + Shift) + E key

Merge Visible command

Flattening an Image (Flattening All Layers)

To flatten an image (merge all layers into the background), choose Layer > Flatten Image, or select Flatten Image from the palette menu.

Flatten Image command

Preserving a Layer's Transparency

You can make it so that only non-transparent (areas of a layer containing image data) can be edited by checking the Preserve Transparency option. This eliminates the need to purposely select the non-transparent areas of the image for each edit. To activate or deactivate this function, select the layer on the Layers palette and click Preserve Transparency. This option cannot be used on the background layer.

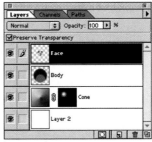

Layers palette

GRADIENT SETTINGS

Select a Gradient tool corresponding to the shape to be filled from the toolbox. To specify the gradient, click at the point where you wish it to start and drag to the end point (release mouse button). If a selected area is not specified, the gradient fill will be applied to the whole active layer. Set the gradient options by double-clicking the selected Gradient tool to display the Options palette. Set the opacity and paint mode.

Linear Gradient Tool

Angle Gradient Tool

Diamond Gradient Tool

Gradient Tools
Photoshop 5.0 supports new gradient styles

Radial Gradient Tool

Reflected Gradient Tool

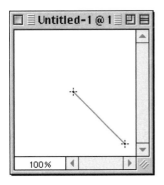

Creating Gradient Styles

Create a new gradient style by clicking Edit on the Gradient Tool Options palette to display the Gradient Editor. Select New and enter a name for the gradient. Define the style by adjusting the color boxes, transparency, location, and other settings. Dragging the color boxes and specifying the colors can create a multicolor gradient. To specify or change colors, double click the color box to display the Color Picker dialog box and make changes.

Gradient Tool Options palette

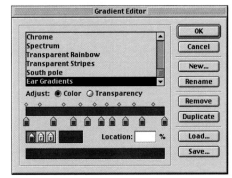

Gradient Editor dialog box

Loading and Saving Gradient Styles

To load a gradient style, click the Load button in the Gradient Editor dialog box. Specify the gradient file and click Open. The new gradient will load and appear at the bottom of the gradient list. To save a new gradient style as a file, select it from the list, click Save on the Gradient Editor and enter a file name.

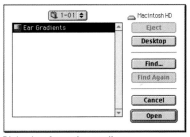

Dialog box for saving gradients.

The History palette is equipped with tools for reversing deletions and image edits performed in multiple steps. A new state of the image is added to the list each time a change is applied. The earliest state is displayed at the top of the history palette list and the most recent at the bottom. You can return to any state and display or revise it.

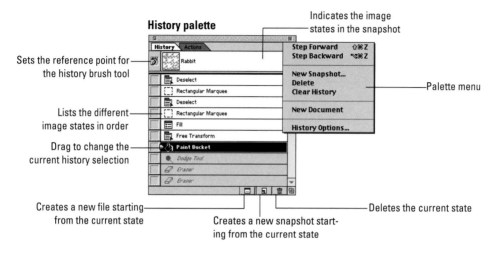

History palette

Indicates the image states in the snapshot

Sets the reference point for the history brush tool

Lists the different image states in order

Drag to change the current history selection

Palette menu

Creates a new file starting from the current state

Creates a new snapshot starting from the current state

Deletes the current state

Deleting Image States

To delete a given state and all subsequent states, click on it in the History palette and select Delete from the palette menu or drag it onto the trash can.

Clearing the History Palette

To clear the history palette without changing the current image, select Erase History from the palette menu.

Setting Options

To set the history palette options, select History Options from the palette menu. You can specify such settings as the maximum number of recordable states in the palette and whether or not the first snapshot is saved.

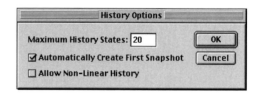

The actions function records multiple steps as one action to automate processes. This is extremely useful in processing several files at once or for repeating the same series of commands on a single file. Starting with Photoshop 5.0, actions can be collected in folders and made into sets. Version 5.0 also features more recordable operations and enhanced functionality than previous versions.

Action palette

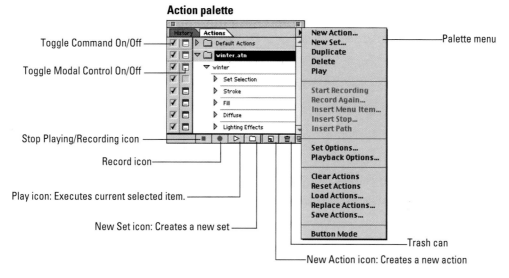

Toggle Command On/Off
Toggle Modal Control On/Off
Stop Playing/Recording icon
Record icon
Play icon: Executes current selected item.
New Set icon: Creates a new set
Palette menu
Trash can
New Action icon: Creates a new action

Creating a New Action

To create a new action, select New Action from the palette menu. Enter a name in the New Action dialog box and click Record to commence recording. When all steps are recorded, click the Stop Playing/Recording icon on the palette menu to stop recording. The newly recorded action will appear at the bottom of the action list.

Playing an Action

To play a recorded action, click a command or set of commands on the Actions palette, then choose Play from the palette menu, or click the Play icon at the bottom of the palette menu. If you click the Display Dialog box to 'On', you can adjust the settings as required for each action being played.

Loading an Action

To load a recorded action, select Load Action from the Actions palette menu. Select the action file then click Open to add the selected action to the Actions palette.

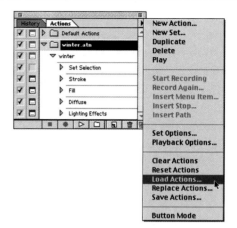

Saving and Editing an Action

To facilitate viewing of the palette list, Photoshop 5.0 and future versions enable related operations to be collected in a folder to create a set. To create a new set, select New Set from the palette menu. Type a name then press OK to create a new folder in the Actions palette. The palette can then be rearranged by dragging and dropping existing actions into the folder. Release the mouse button when the highlighted line indicates the target folder.

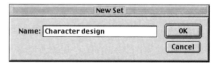

A path refers to a line drawn on an image file using the Pen tool. As the path itself is not an image, it will not be printed with the image, but it can be filled to create a line drawing or it can be converted to a selection border. A path is displayed as a Bezier curve like those used in other software programs, such as Illustrator.

Paths palette

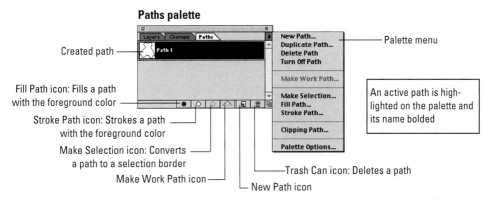

Created path

Fill Path icon: Fills a path with the foreground color

Stroke Path icon: Strokes a path with the foreground color

Make Selection icon: Converts a path to a selection border

Make Work Path icon

New Path icon

Trash Can icon: Deletes a path

Palette menu

An active path is highlighted on the palette and its name bolded

Path Tools

 Pen Tool
Click the Pen tool to create anchor points used as control points to draw a smooth curve.

 Magnetic Pen Tool
Drag the Magnetic Pen tool around the perimeter of an object to draw a path that snaps to the edges.

 Freeform Pen Tool
Drag the Freeform Pen tool to draw a freehand path. Anchor points are automatically created at the appropriate positions.

 Add-Anchor-Point Tool
Click the Add-Anchor-Point tool on a path created with the Pen tool to add an anchor point.

 Delete-Anchor-Point Tool
Click the Delete-Anchor-Point tool on an anchor point created with the Pen tool to delete it.

 Direct-Selection Tool
Click the Direct-Selection tool on an anchor point to select it to edit the direction lines or other attributes. It can also be dragged to select multiple anchor points as a subpath.

 Convert-Anchor-Point Tool
Convert a path from smooth points (both direction lines lie along the same angle and move together) to corner points (each direction line can be modified independently) or vice versa.

Showing Paths

Select the path in the Paths palette. The path is displayed on the image file where it can be selected or moved.

A path selected on the Paths palette is shown on the image.

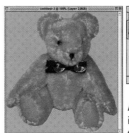

A path will not appear on the image unless it is selected on the Paths palette.

Drawing Paths

To create a new path, select the Pen tool from the toolbox. A path drawn on an image is automatically saved into the Paths palette as a temporary work path. Work paths can be erased by clicking a clear area of the Paths palette and redrawn as often as needed. To create and save a new path, select New Path from the palette menu and specify a name in the New Path dialog box.

New Path dialog box

Shortcut	Click on the New Path icon.

Saving Paths

Select the work path on the Paths palette, then choose Save Path from the Paths palette menu. Enter a name for the path in the dialog box and click OK. The path will be saved into the Paths palette. Use the Direct-Selection tool to select any stored path for use. Selected paths can be used as a subpath.

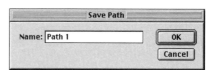

Save Path dialog box

Converting Selection Borders to Paths

To convert a selection border to a path, select Make Work Path from the palette menu, then set the tolerance value and click OK in the dialog box. The lower the tolerance value, the greater the number of anchor points and the more detailed the path.

Shortcut	Click the Make Work Path icon on the Paths palette.

This selection border is converted to a path.

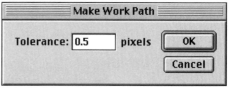

Make Work Path dialog box

Converting Paths to Selection Borders

Select the path on the Paths palette, then choose Make Selection from the palette menu. Enter values for the Feather Radius and the Selection options. If there is a current selection, specify whether the path is to be added to or subtracted from the original selection, or if an area common to both the path and the original selection is to be selected.

Shortcut Command-click (Ctrl-click) the path name to convert the path to a selection border. Or, click the Make Selection icon on the Paths palette.

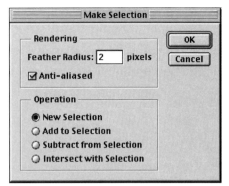

Make Selection dialog box. The drawn path is converted to a selection border.

Painting a Path Border (Stroking a Path)

Select the path to be stroked on the Paths palette. Select the foreground color as the color for the border and specify the brush size in the Brushes palette. Choose Stroke Path from the Paths palette menu and select the tool to be used for stroking. Click OK to paint a path border.

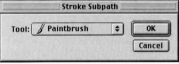

Stroke Path dialog box. Select a tool and click OK to paint the path border automatically

Shortcut If the foreground color and brush size have already been set, click the Stroke Path icon on the Paths palette.

Moving Paths between Images

To move a path to another image file, select the path on the Paths palette and drag and drop the selected path onto the desired image file.

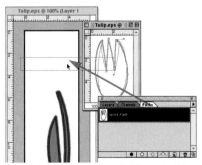

Dragging and dropping a path. The path of the Tulip image is moved to the Stem and Leaf image.

To make Photoshop more user-friendly, the screen display, Save options, pointer appearance, ruler units, and other Preferences settings can be customized. Refer to the Photoshop User Guide for details.

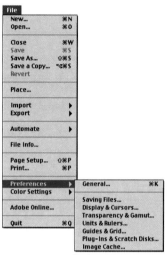

Preferences menu

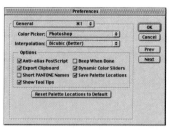

Preferences dialog box: Click 'Previous' or 'Next' to access another Preferences menu without closing the dialog box.

DRAWING WITH PATTERNS

If you are one of those people resigned to the fact that you are not artistic, Photoshop has come to the rescue. Using the power of your computer you can create illustrations from circular and angular designs without a ruler or compass. Artwork deemed beyond the realm of an amateur can be created in an instant by combining elements and applying filters. There is nothing in this chapter that requires freehand drawing skills. All images can be produced using simple tools like the Rectangular or Elliptical Marquee tools. More sophisticated tools, such as gradients and filters, will add shading and texture to create images rivaling those of professional computer graphic artists.

CREATING AN ILLUSTRATION USING POLAR COORDINATES

A disk of extremely fine lines that appear virtually impossible to draw by hand can be easily sketched by applying a combination of filters to a blank file. Try your hand at creating a porcupine with this technique.

1

Create a new file that is 800 x 800 pixels. Set the Resolution to 72 ppi and the Contents to Transparent. First you will make a disk with spines to represent the porcupine's body. Use the Channels palette to create a new channel (Alpha Channel 1). Select about 90% of the full image with the Rectangular Marquee tool as indicated in the diagram. Choose Filter > Noise > Add Noise. Set the Amount to '999,' Distribution to Uniform, and place a check in the Grayscale checkbox. Apply the filter. Deselect the selection.

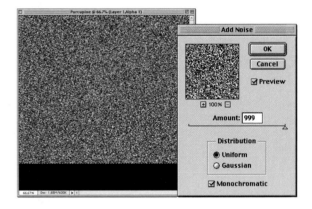

2

Choose Filter > Blur > Motion Blur. Set the Angle to -90° and Distance to 150 pixels. Apply the filter.

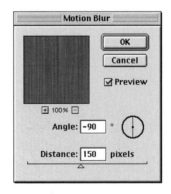

3

Choose Filter > Other > Offset. Set the Horizontal option to 0 pixels and the Vertical to -50 pixels. Set Undefined Areas to 'Repeat Edge Pixels' to equalize the image. Apply the filter. Choose Image > Adjust > Invert.

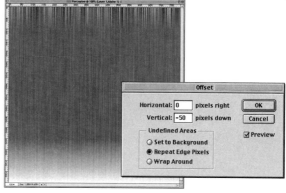

4

Choose Image > Adjust > Levels. Set the levels as indicated in the diagram to increase the contrast.

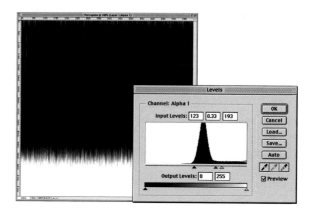

5

Return to the RGB channel. Rename Layer 1 'Body.' Choose Select > Load Selection. Set the Channel to 'Alpha Channel 1' and place a check in the Invert checkbox. Click OK to load the selection. Fill in the selection with purple (R:39, G:0, B:49). Deselect the selection.

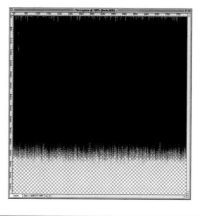

6

Choose Filter > Distort > Polar Coordinates. Set the Convert option to 'Rectangular to Polar.' Click OK to apply the filter to the painted image. And there's your prickly disk.

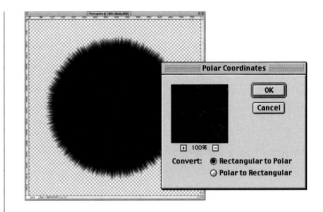

7

To give depth to the image in Step 6, you will make a cone and combine the two. Create a new layer named 'Cone.' Return the foreground and background to the default colors. Choose the Linear Gradient tool in the toolbox. Set the options as shown in the diagram, and drag the tool from the bottom right to the top left.

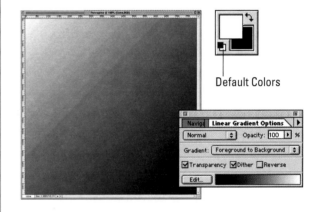

8

Choose Filter > Distort > Pinch. Set the Amount to 100% and click OK. Hold down command (Ctrl) and type F several times to repeat the effect. The image gradually transforms to a cone as viewed from above. The command was repeated 8 times to achieve the effect in this diagram.

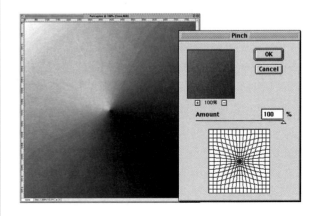

9

You will now create a composite of the cone created in Step 8 and the prickly disk. Leave the 'Cone' layer active and command-click (Ctrl-click) the 'Body' layer on the Layers palette to load the selection. Choose Layer > Add Layer Mask > Reveal Selection. Portions of the cone image extending outside the Body image will be removed. Move the 'Cone' layer below the 'Body' layer on the Layers palette. Set the blending mode for the 'Body' layer to Multiply. You have now given the prickly disk some depth.

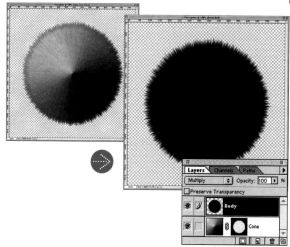

10

Next you will color the porcupine's stomach. Select the 'Body' layer and select an area for the stomach with the Elliptical Marquee tool. Choose Select > Feather and set the Feather Radius to 10 pixels. Choose Image > Adjust > Hue/Saturation. Place a check in the Colorize checkbox and adjust the settings to the diagram to change the selection's color. Deselect the selection.

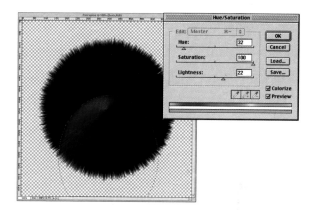

11

You will now make the porcupine's ears. First, create a new file that is 200 x 200 pixels. Choose the Radial Gradient tool from the toolbox and click Edit on the Gradient Tool Options palette to display the Gradient Editor. Click Load, then open Image > 1-01 > 'ear.grd' on the supplementary CD-ROM. Set the options to the diagram values and drag the tool straight down from the center of the image.

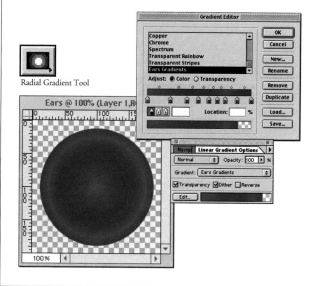

Radial Gradient Tool

12

Copy the ear image and paste it onto the prickly disk. Name the newly formed layer 'Ear.' Choose the Move tool and then Edit > Free Transform to change the ear to an appropriate size. Move the ear to the desired position.

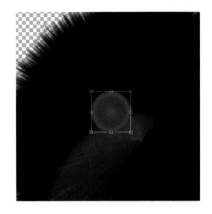

13

Choose Select > Load Selection and set the Channel to 'Ear Transparency' in the Load Selection dialog box. Choose Layer > Add Layer Mask > Reveal Selection. On the Channels palette, turn on the eye icon for 'Ear mask' and make it active. Set the Linear Gradient tool to the values shown in the diagram and drag as indicated. Select the 'Ear' layer on the Layers palette and choose Layer > Delete Layer Mask. Click Apply in the dialog box to apply the mask before deletion.

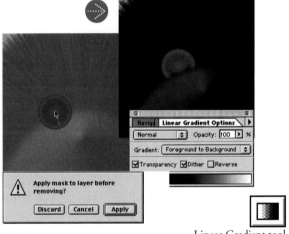

Linear Gradient tool

14

Duplicate the completed 'Ear' layer by choosing Layer > Duplicate Layer. Choose Edit > Transform > Flip Horizontal. Adjust the location of the respective ears with the Move tool.

15

You will create the eyes next. First, create a new file named 'Eye.' Hold down shift (Shift) and draw a circle the size of an eye using the Elliptical Marquee tool. Return the foreground and background to the default colors and switch them. Choose the Radial Gradient tool and set the options to the diagram values. Drag the tool inside the circle from the top left to the bottom right.

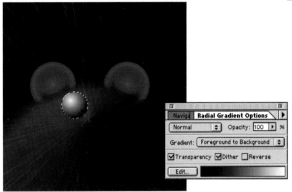

16

Use the Elliptical Marquee tool to draw a smaller circle inside the previous circle. Using the procedure used for the first circle, create a black pupil by selecting the Radial Gradient tool and dragging it inside the circle from the top left to the bottom right, this time for a shorter distance. When one eye is complete, duplicate the eye in another layer and use the Move tool to position both eyes.

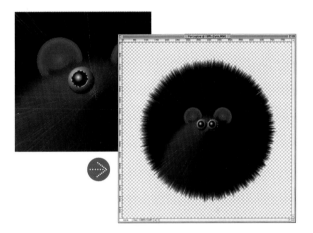

17

Now you will make the mouth. Create a new file of about 300 x 300 pixels. Reset the foreground and background to the default colors and switch them. Drag the Linear Gradient tool diagonally from the top left to the bottom right as you did in Steps 7 and 8. Create a cone using the Pinch filter. Choose Image > Adjust > Hue/Saturation. Place a check in the Colorize checkbox in the dialog box. Adjust the settings as indicated in the diagram and color the image.

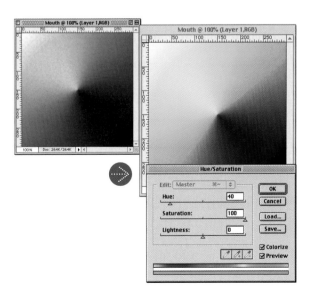

18

Hold down the option (Alt) key and select an oval with the Elliptical Marquee tool starting from the center of the image. Copy the image and paste it into the 'Porcupine' file. Choose Edit > Free Transform to flatten the oval by dragging the upper and lower middle handles slightly inward.

19

Now for the nose. Create a new layer named 'Nose.' Hold down the shift (Shift) key and draw a small circle with the Elliptical Marquee tool. Change the foreground color to white and the background to pink (R:185, G:0, B:77). Choose the Radial Gradient tool and set the options to the diagram values. Drag the tool inside the circle from the top left to the bottom right to apply the gradient and give the nose depth.

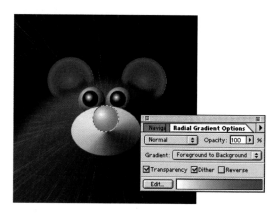

20

Finally, you will create the whiskers. Create a new file named 'Whisker.' Use the Rectangular Marquee tool to draw a narrow rectangle. Change the foreground color to light green (R:148, G:190, B:37) and the background to dark green (R:24, G:61, B:33). Choose the Linear Gradient tool, set the options to the diagram values, then hold down the shift (Shift) key and drag the tool from the top of the rectangle to the bottom. Choose Edit > Free Transform to transform the rectangle into a line.

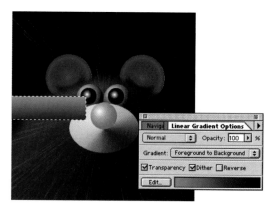

21

Duplicate the 'Whisker' layer twice to make three lines. Choose Edit > Transform > Rotate. Tilt the top and bottom lines up and down, respectively, by approximately 15 degrees. Merge the three 'Whisker' layers into one, select the resulting layer and then duplicate it. Choose Edit > Transform > Flip Horizontal. Use the Move tool to adjust the position of the whiskers. Congratulations, the porcupine is now complete.

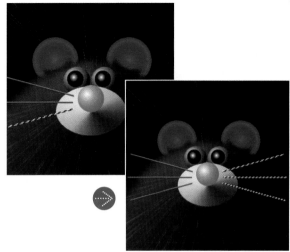

CREATING THREE-DIMENSIONAL SHADOWS WITH CHANNELS

It is easy to create images that look as if they were created with 3-D software by applying three-dimensional shadows and blurring techniques. The key is to apply blurring separately to different parts of the image.

1

Create a new file that is 500 x 500 pixels. Set the Resolution to 72 ppi and the Contents to Transparent. Create a new layer above 'Layer 1' and name it 'Ears.' Draw an ear-shaped selection with the Elliptical Marquee tool. Set the foreground color to white and fill the ellipse with white. Deselect the selection. Select another ellipse inside the first and fill it with pink (R:221, G:113, B:163).

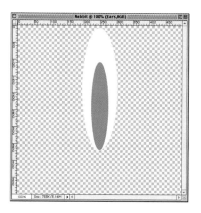

2

Deselect the selection.

Choose Edit > Transform > Numeric and set Rotate to -15°. Select the whole image, hold down command + option (Ctrl + Alt) and drag and copy the image to make the other ear. With the new ear still selected, choose Edit > Transform > Flip Horizontal. Adjust the positions of the ears.

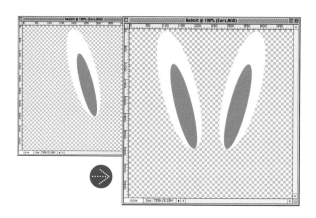

3

Create a new layer named 'Face.' Draw an oval with the Elliptical Marquee tool to make the face selection. Fill it with white. Deselect the selection.

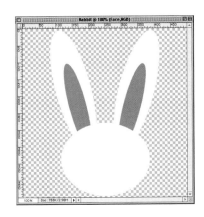

4

Create a new layer named 'Eyes.' Draw one eye with the Elliptical Marquee tool. Fill it with pink (R:234, G:164, B:194). Place a check in the Preserve Transparency checkbox in the Layers palette to protect the area outside the pink eye. Choose the Elliptical Marquee tool and draw a circle on top of the pink eye. This will be the eyeball. Fill it with black.

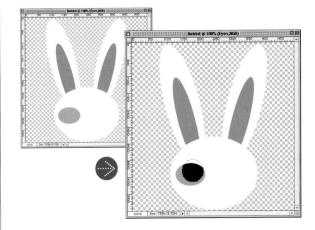

5

Deselect the selection. Choose Edit > Transform > Numeric and set Rotate to 10°. Select the whole image, hold down command + option (Ctrl + Alt) and drag and copy the image to make the other eye. With the new eye still selected, choose Edit > Transform > Flip Horizontal.

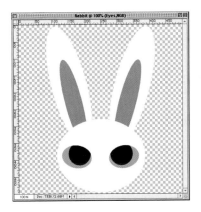

6

Create a new file named 'Mouth.' Draw a circle with the Elliptical Marquee tool. Fill it with white. When one circle is complete, leave it selected, hold down command + option (Ctrl + Alt) and drag and copy the image to make another mouth. Align the two mouths symmetrically side-by-side. It is best to hide the 'Face' layer since the white mouth is difficult to see on top of the white face.

7

Create a new file named 'Nose.'
Draw an oval with the Elliptical Marquee tool. This is to be the nose. Fill it with red (R:255, G:0, B:0).

8

Next, we'll do some hair. Create a new file that is 100 x 100 pixels and set the Contents to Transparent. Using the Pen tool, draw a closed path resembling a water drop as in the diagram. Convert the path to a selection border and fill it with light gray (R:229, G:229, B:229). Deselect the selection. Choose Filter > Distort >Twirl and set the Angle to 150°.

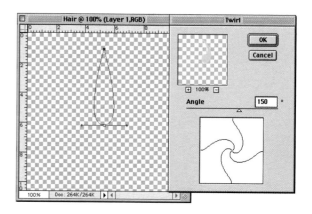

9

Copy and paste this image onto the image of the Rabbit. Transform the result with Edit > Free Transform and position it with the Move tool. Name the newly formed layer 'Hair 1.' Repeat these steps to make six or seven 'Hair' layers.

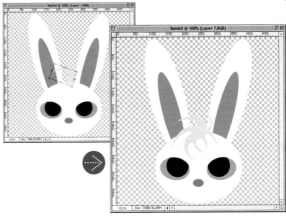

10

Add shadows to these images to create a quasi 3-D effect. Select the 'Face' layer on the Layers palette to make it active, then command-click (Ctrl-click) it to load the selection. Choose Select > Save Selection. Save the selection into a new channel named 'Face.' Deselect the selection. Click on the 'Face' channel to make it the active channel. Choose Filter > Blur > Gaussian Blur and set the Radius to 15 pixels.

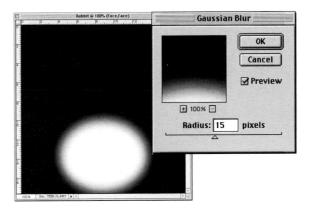

11

Select RGB as the active channel. Choose Filter > Render > Lighting Effects. Set the options as shown in the diagram. Apply the filter to see the image assume a quasi 3-D appearance.

12

Create channels for the eyes, mouth, nose and hair, and apply the lighting effect to each to produce quasi 3-D effects as you did for the face. However, apply different Radius values for the Gaussian Blur filter to each channel as follows: eye: 7 pixels, mouth: 6 pixels, nose: 6 pixels and the hair: 4 pixels. When applying the Lighting Effects filter, set the Texture channel at the bottom of the Lighting Effects dialog box to the respective channels.

13

The procedures are slightly different for the ears. Select the 'Ear' layer as the active layer and hide all the other layers in the Layers palette by clicking off the eye icons. Load the transparent area of the 'Ear' layer with Selection > Load Selection, setting the Channel to 'Ear Transparency.' Hold down the command + shift + option (Ctrl + Shift + Alt) keys and click the RGB channel on the Channels palette. Save the new selection and create a new 'Ear' channel. Select the 'Ear' channel as the active channel. Deselect the selection. Choose Filter > Blur > Gaussian Blur and set the Radius to 8 pixels. Return to the RGB channel and apply Filter > Render > Lighting Effects.

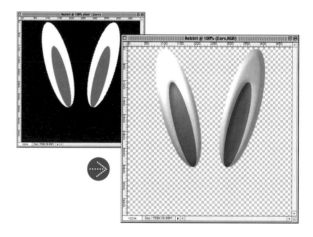

14

Next, mold the mouth into the face. Insert eye icons into all layers in the Layers palette to show them. Select the 'Mouth' layer to make it active and load its selection. Choose Layer > Add Layer Mask > Reveal Selection. Display the Channels palette. Since the 'Mouth mask' is active, click off all eye icons except for the 'Mouth mask.'

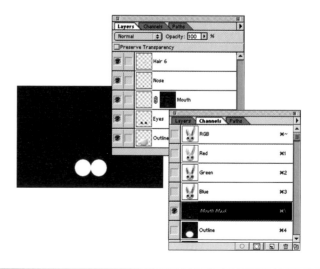

15

Choose the Linear Gradient tool and set the blending mode to 'Multiply' and the Gradient to 'Black, White.' Start dragging about 1/4 of the way down from the top of the mouth to its bottom edge as shown in the diagram. Return to the RGB channel. The face and mouth will be molded together.

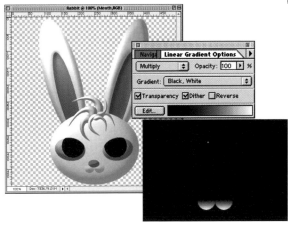

16

Now you should add some reflected light to the eyes and nose. Select the 'Eye' layer to make it active. Choose a soft-edged brush of an appropriate size to apply shading. A 21-pixel Airbrush tool was used to create the diagram shown. Click the brush on the desired area. Repeat the procedure on the nose. The character is now complete.

17

The last step is to create the background. Change the name of 'Layer 1' at the bottom of the Layers palette to 'Background.' Fill it with white. Choose Filter > Noise > Add Noise. Set the Amount to 999 and place a check in the Monochromatic checkbox. Click OK.

18

Choose Filter > Blur > Gaussian Blur and set the Radius to 2 pixels. Click OK.

19

Choose Filter > Distort > Ocean Ripple. Set Ripple Size and Ripple Magnitude each to 9. Click OK.

20

Choose Filter > Stylize > Emboss. Set the Angle to 135°, the Height to 2 pixels and the Amount to 340%. Click OK.

21

Choose Image > Adjust > Hue/Saturation. Place a check in the Colorize checkbox and set the values to those in the diagram. Click OK. This completes the illustration.

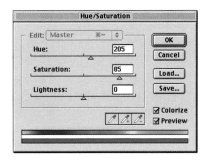

CREATING FIGURES USING GRADIENTS

Three-dimensional figures can be created with gradients and tools alone. We have prepared gradient files to make it easier for you.

1

Create a new file that is 500 x 500 pixels. Set the Resolution to 72 ppi and the Contents to Transparent. Choose the Radial Gradient tool and click Edit on the Gradient Tool Options palette to display the Gradient Editor. Click Load, then open Image > 1-03 > 'snowman.grd' on the supplementary CD-ROM. Set the blending mode to Lighten.

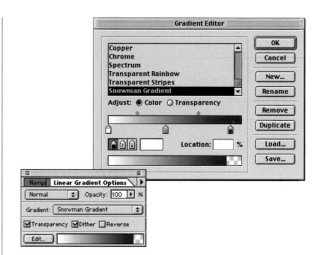

2

Choose the Radial Gradient tool and set the options to the diagram values. Drag it slightly farther than the radius of the circles to produce spheres with a blue tint. Apply the gradient first to the head, then drag it over the body to overlap the head. This will fuse the two spheres together. Name the layer 'Body.'

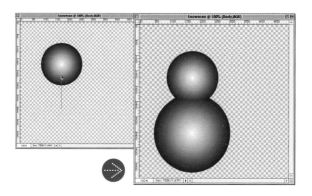

3

Create a new layer named 'Eyes.' Set the foreground and background to the default colors and switch them. Draw a small circle with the Elliptical Marquee tool where an eye is to be placed. Drag the Radial Gradient tool from the top left to the center of the circle with the options set to the diagram values. Keep the circle selected and choose the Move tool. Hold down the command + option (Ctrl + Alt) keys and drag and copy it to create the other eye.

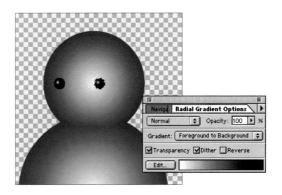

4

Create a new file that is 300 x 300 pixels and set the Contents to Transparent. Draw a rectangle with the Rectangular Marquee tool similar in size to the one in the diagram. Set the foreground color to white and the background to orange (R:197, G:107, B:0). Choose the Linear Gradient tool, set the options to the diagram values and drag the tool from the top of the rectangle to the bottom. Select the entire image. Choose Layer > Align to Selection > Vertical Center, then choose Layer > Align to Selection > Left Edge.

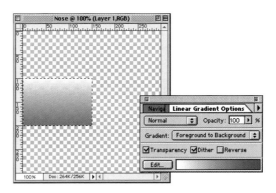

5

Choose Edit > Transform > Perspective, then drag the top left anchor point downward to make a trapezoid. Choose Filter > Distort > Shear. Set the shear graph as shown in the diagram. Apply the filter to transform the image to a cone.

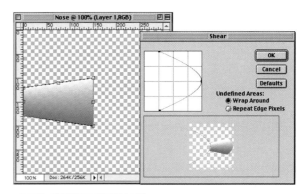

6

Draw an oval with the Elliptical Marquee tool to match the front tip of the cone. Choose the Linear Gradient tool and drag it from the bottom right to the top left of the oval. This completes the nose.

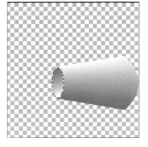

7

Select the whole 'Nose' image. Copy and paste it onto the 'Snowman' image. Choose Edit > Transform > Distort to adjust the size and placement as desired.

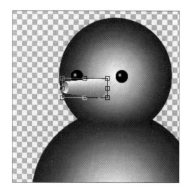

8

Next you will make the bucket. Create a new file that is 300 x 300 pixels and set the Contents to Transparent. Draw a rectangle with the Rectangular Marquee tool about the size of the one in the diagram. Set the foreground color to white and the background to red (R:238, G:15, B:15). Choose the Linear Gradient tool and set the options to the diagram values. Drag the tool from the bottom to the top of the rectangle. Select the entire image and align the image along the vertical center and right edge with the procedures used in Step 4.

9

Choose Edit > Transform > Perspective and make a trapezoid with the procedures used for the nose. Choose Filter > Distort > Shear. Set the shear graph as shown in the diagram. Apply the filter to transform the image.

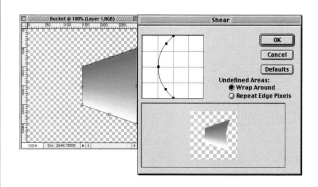

10

Copy the image of the bucket and paste it onto the Snowman image. Choose Edit > Transform > Distort and adjust the bucket so that the Snowman appears to be wearing the bucket on its head.

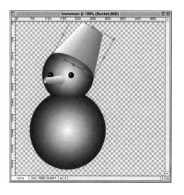

11

Next create a new layer named 'Mouth.' Draw a rectangle with the Rectangular Marquee tool approximately where the mouth would be placed and fill it with brown (R:68, G:50, B:33). Duplicate the 'Mouth' layer. Choose Filter > Stylize > Emboss, set the values to those in the diagram and click OK to apply the filter to the 'Mouth Copy' layer. On the Layers palette, set the blending mode to Multiply.

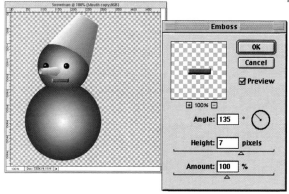

12

You will now add texture to the snowman's body. Select the 'Body' layer to make it active. Choose Layer > New Layer > Layer. Name the new layer 'Texture.' Set the Mode to Soft Light and place a check in the Group with Previous Layer checkbox.

13

Choose Filter > Render > Clouds Pattern 1. Click OK. Choose Filter > Stylize > Emboss. Set the values to those in the diagram and click OK.

14

One Snowman is now complete. Choose Image > Duplicate to make a copy. Choose Image > Adjust > Hue/Saturation for each of the bucket, nose and body layers, and adjust the Hue slider to the colors of your preference.

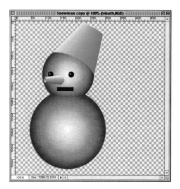

15

Choose Layer > Merge Visible. Then copy and paste it onto the original image. Choose Edit > Free Transform and change the size of the second snowman. Choose Layer > Merge Visible to merge the snowmen layers, and name the result 'Snowmen.'

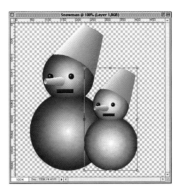

16

Create a new layer and name it 'Background.' Move it below the 'Snowmen' layer in the Layers palette. Choose the Linear Gradient tool. Set the foreground color to light blue (R:0, G:255, B:255) and the background to white. Apply the gradient, as shown in the diagram, from the top of the image to the bottom.

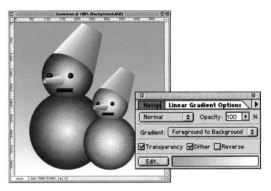

17

Create a new layer called 'Snow' and move it to the very top of the stack. Set the foreground color to white. Choose the Airbrush tool. Set the Pressure to 80% and scatter snowflakes using three brush sizes with diameters of 35, 45, and 65 pixels, respectively.

18

Lastly, add the shadows. Create a new layer named 'Shadow' above the 'Background' layer. Hold down the command (Ctrl) key and click on the 'Snowmen' layer to load its selection. Fill it with navy blue (R:20, G:25, B:65). Choose Edit > Transform > Distort and modify as indicated in the diagram.

19

Deselect the selection. Choose Filter > Blur > Gaussian Blur and set the Radius to 5 pixels. Click OK to apply the filter and complete the illustration.

PROVIDING DEPTH
WITH GRADIENTS

In this exercise, you will use gradients to apply shadows to a cylinder to make it appear more three-dimensional. You will also learn to make effective use of perspective.

1

Create a new file that is 500 x 500 pixels. Set the Resolution to 72 ppi and the Contents to Transparent. Draw an oval with the Elliptical Marquee tool toward the bottom of the screen. This oval will become the base of the mailbox. Set the foreground color to red (R:255, G:0, B:0) and fill the selection.

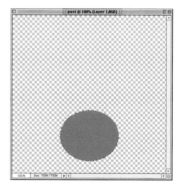

2

Draw a rectangle of the same width as the oval in Step 1 with the Rectangular Marquee tool, and fill it with red. Position the rectangle on the top half of the oval.

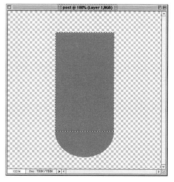

3

Hold down the command (Ctrl) key and click on 'Layer 1' in the Layers palette to load its selection. Set the foreground color to black. Choose the Linear Gradient tool. Set the options to the diagram values and apply the gradient from the selection's right edge toward the center. Do the same from the left edge.

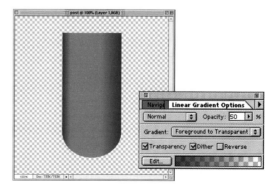

4

Choose Select > Select All, then center the mailbox in the center of the screen by choosing Edit > Cut and Edit > Paste.

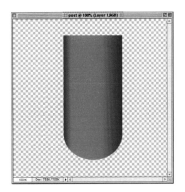

5

Create a new layer. Draw a square with the Rectangular Marquee tool to make the mailbox door. Fill it with red. Set the foreground color to black and apply a gradient from the right bottom to the top left of the selection using the same settings as in Step 3. Center the selection in the screen using the cut and paste technique. Choose the Move tool, hold down the shift (Shift) key and move the door down to an appropriate position.

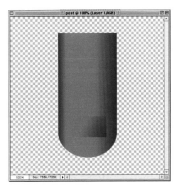

6

Keep 'Layer 2' active and choose Layer > Effects > Drop Shadow. Set the values to those in the diagram and add a shadow to the door.

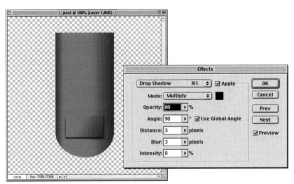

7

Choose Layer > Merge Visible to merge the two layers. Name the layer 'Body.' Deselect the selection. Choose Edit > Transform > Perspective and narrow the lower portion of the body as indicated in the diagram.

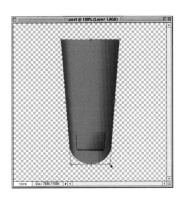

8

Create a new layer above the 'Body' layer. Draw an oval slightly larger than the body with the Elliptical Marquee tool as shown in the diagram. Fill it with red first, then set the foreground to black with Opacity set to 50% and fill it again. Cut and paste to position the image at the center of the screen. Choose the Move tool, hold down the shift (Shift) key and move the oval up.

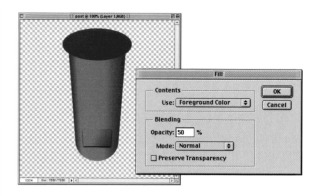

9

Create a new layer above 'Layer 1' to add shading. Hold down the command (Ctrl) key and click on 'Layer 1' to create a selection. Choose Select > Modify > Contract and set the Contract By box to 10 pixels.

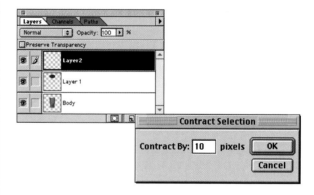

10

Choose the Rectangular Marquee tool and move the selection 5 pixels upward using the keyboard cursor key. Choose Select > Feather and set the Feather Radius to 5 pixels. Fill the selection with red. Merge 'Layer 1' and 'Layer 2' and rename the result 'Roof.'

11

Keep the 'Roof' layer active and select the entire roof image. Hold down option + shift (Alt + Shift) and move the image up with the Move tool to duplicate the roof within the same layer. Choose Edit > Copy to copy the selection.

12

Deselect the selection, then paste. To create a protruding ridge around the body, choose Edit > Transform > Scale. Hold down option (Alt) and contract the ridge until it protrudes only slightly from the body.

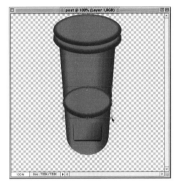

13

Load the 'Layer 1' selection. Choose Select > Modify > Contract, and set the Contract By box to 5 pixels. Choose a selection tool and move the selection up with a cursor key, then press the delete (Backspace) key to delete it. Make the 'Body' layer active, link it with 'Layer 1' and merge the two.

14

Create another new layer right above the 'Body' layer. Create a selection with the Elliptical Marquee tool to serve as the slot of the mailbox. Fill it with red. Set the foreground color to black. Choose the Linear Gradient tool, set the options to the diagram values and apply the gradient from the bottom right of the circle to the top left.

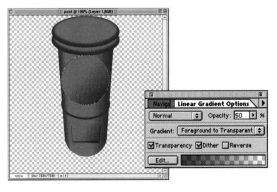

15

Choose Select > Modify > Contract and set the Contract By box to 10 pixels Choose the Rectangular Marquee tool and shift the selection 3 pixels down with the keyboard cursor. Choose Select > Feather. Set the Feather Radius to 2 pixels and fill the selection with red. Deselect the selection.

16

Duplicate 'Layer 1' and create a 'Layer 1 copy.' Choose Edit > Transform > Scale and reduce the size slightly as shown in the diagram. Use the Move tool to shift the circle to the appropriate position.

17

Choose Edit > Transform > Rotate 180°. Load the 'Layer 1 copy' selection. Set the foreground color to black. Choose the Linear Gradient tool. Set the options to the diagram values and apply the gradient from the top of the circle to the center. Do NOT deselect the selection.

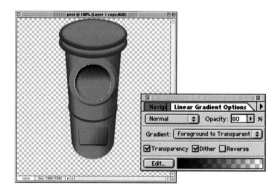

18

Create a new layer above 'Layer 1 copy.' Make 'Layer 2' active, choose Select > Modify > Contract, and set the Contract By box to 3 pixels. Fill the selection with red. Set the foreground color to black and use the same settings as in Step 3 to apply the gradient from the bottom right up to the top left of the selected circle.

19

On the Layers palette, hold down the command (Ctrl) key and click on the 'Roof' layer to load its selection into 'Layer 2.' Hold down the shift (Shift) key and use the keyboard cursor to move the oval down so that it appears to form a brim around the upper part of the slot as shown in the diagram. Choose Select > Inverse and press the delete (Backspace) key. Link the three layers, merge them and give the result the name 'Slot.'

20

Set the foreground color to white. Choose the Text tool and type 'POST.' Choose a font and text size appropriate to the image size. Position the text at the bottom of the cover.

21

Choose Layer > Effects > Drop Shadow. Set the values to those in the diagram and click OK.

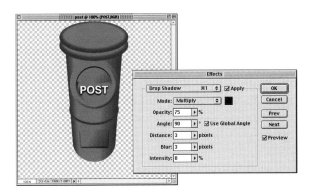

22

Create a new layer named 'Base' and move it below the 'Body' layer. Create a selection with the Elliptical Marquee tool to form the base of the mailbox. Make it slightly wider than the bottom of the body. Fill it with white. Choose Filter > Noise > Add Noise and set the values to those in the diagram.

23

Choose Image > Adjust > Brightness/Contrast. Set the Brightness to -100. Choose Layer > Add Layer Mask > Reveal Selection and click on the 'Base' layer thumbnail.

24

Load the 'Base' layer selection. Choose Select > Modify > Contract and set the Contract By box to 10 pixels. Move the selection 5 pixels up with the keyboard cursor key. Choose Select > Feather. Set the Feather Radius to 5 pixels and fill the selection with white.

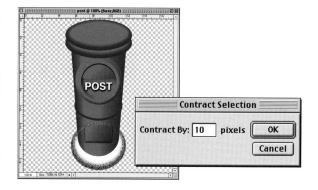

25

Add noise as indicated in the diagram to complete the illustration.

CREATING THE TEXTURE OF REAL WOOD

In this example, you will use the Emboss and Noise filters to create boards that appear to have a real wood grain. You can add to the 3-D illusion by cropping the boards randomly.

1

Create a new file that is 500 x 500 pixels. Set the Resolution to 72 ppi and Contents to White. Choose Filter > Noise > Add Noise. Set the Amount to 300 and the Distribution to Uniform. Place a check in the Grayscale checkbox. Click OK.

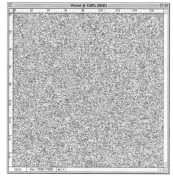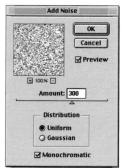

2

Choose Filter > Blur > Motion Blur. Set the Angle to 0° and the Distance to 50 pixels. Click OK.

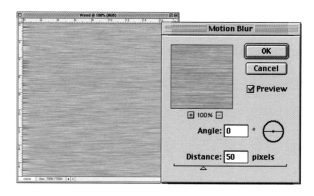

3

Choose Filter > Stylize > Emboss. Set the Angle to 135°, the Height to 2 pixels and the Emboss By box to 50%. The wood grain depth can be adjusted by changing the Height. Click OK.

4

Choose Image > Adjust > Brightness/Contrast. Set the Brightness to 0 and the Contrast to 50. Click OK.

5

Choose Image > Adjust > Color Balance. Set the Midtones to +60, -10, -30 from the left. Set the Highlights to +10, 0, -30. Set the Shadows to +25, 0, -40. Place a check in the Preserve Luminosity checkbox. Click OK.

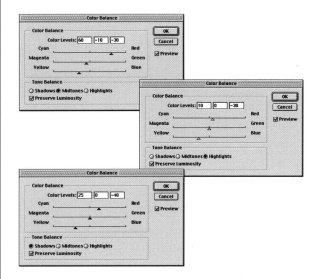

6

Create a new layer named 'Sign Shape.' Create a board shape with the lasso tool. Straight lines can be drawn by holding down the option (Alt) key and dragging the tool in the layer.

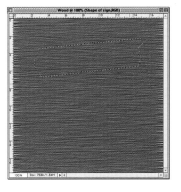

7

Set the foreground to the default color and fill the created selection. Use the same techniques to create two more boards on the same layer.

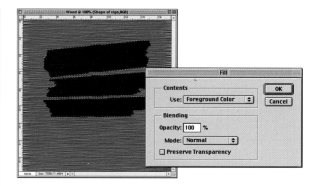

8

Create a new layer named 'Post Shape.' Use the procedures in Step 6 with the lasso tool to create the desired post shape. Fill in the post with the foreground color.

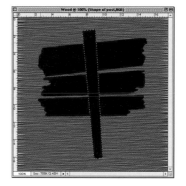

9

Select the 'Background' layer. Hold down the command (Ctrl) key and click on the 'Sign Shape' layer on the Layers palette to load its selection.

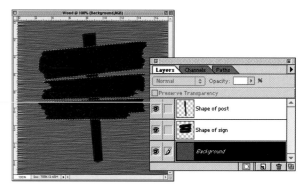

10

Copy and paste the selection from the 'Sign Shape' layer. This will create a new layer (Layer 1) containing the wood grain cut in the shape of the sign above the 'Background' layer. Name the layer 'Sign.'

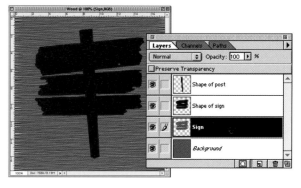

11

Duplicate the 'Background' layer and create a 'Background Copy' layer. Choose Edit > Transform > 90° (Counterclockwise) to rotate the wood grain. Using the procedures from Steps 9 and 10, hold down the command (Ctrl) key and click on the 'Post Shape' layer, and create a new layer using the copy and paste commands. Name the new layer 'Post.'

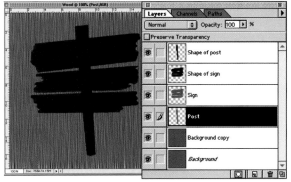

12

Choose Filter > Stylize > Emboss for the 'Post Shape' layer and for the 'Sign Shape' layer. Set the Angle to 135°, the Height to 5 pixels and the Emboss By box to 100%.

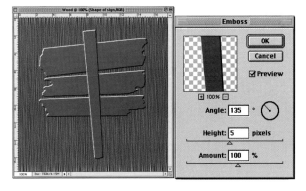

13

Set the blending mode to Overlay for both the 'Post Shape' and 'Sign Shape' layers.

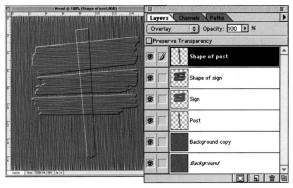

14

Select the 'Sign' layer and link it to the 'Sign Shape' layer. Choose Merge Linked from the Layers Palette menu commands to merge the layers. Use the same procedure to merge the 'Post' and 'Post Shape' layers and the 'Background' and 'Background Copy' layers.

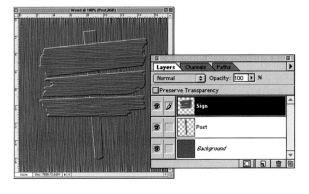

15

Hold down the command (Ctrl) key and click on the 'Post' layer on the Layers palette to load its selection. Choose Layer > Add Layer Mask > Reveal Selection.

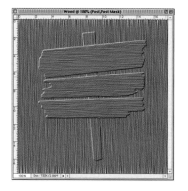

16

Click the 'Post' layer thumbnail, then hold down the command (Ctrl) key and click on the 'Sign' layer on the Layers palette to load its selection. Choose the Move tool and shift the selection down slightly with the cursor key.

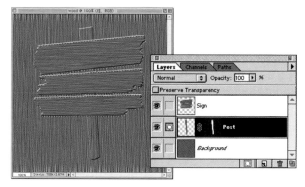

17

Choose Select > Feather and set the Feather Radius to 3 pixels. Click OK. Set the foreground color to black and fill the selection. Deselect the selection.

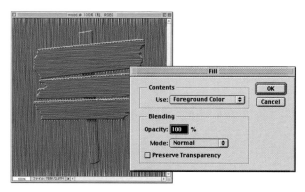

18

Create a new layer above the 'Sign' layer named 'Text.' Set the foreground color to red (R:255, G:0, B:0). Choose the Paintbrush tool and write text that will fit in the wooden signboards. The line width and hardness can be adjusted with the Brushes palette. Set the blending mode to Overlay.

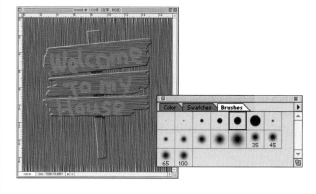

19

Select the 'Text' layer and hold down the command (Ctrl) key and click on the 'Sign' layer to load the selection. Choose Select > Inverse. Press the delete (Backspace) key to remove the color spilling outside the wooden boards.

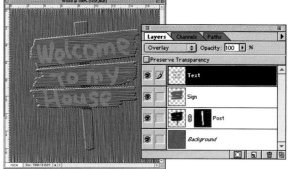

20

Create a new layer called 'Nails' above the 'Text' layer. Use the Elliptical Marquee tool to create a small circular selection. Choose the Radial Gradient tool. Set the foreground color to white and the background to black. Set the options to the diagram values. Apply the gradient from the top of the selected circle just left of center and drag down to the bottom right.

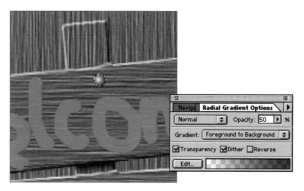

21

Choose Image > Adjust > Brightness/ Contrast. Set the Brightness to 0 and the Contrast to 50. Choose the Move tool. Make two copies of the circle by dragging the selected circle while holding down the option (Alt) key.

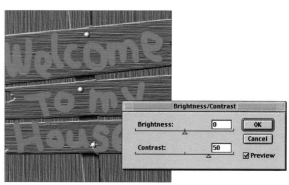

22

Hide the 'Background' layer. Choose Merge Visible from the Layers palette menu to merge the visible layers. Rename the layer 'Wooden Sign.' Choose Image > Adjust > Brightness/Contrast. Set the Brightness to 0 and the Contrast to 10. Click OK.

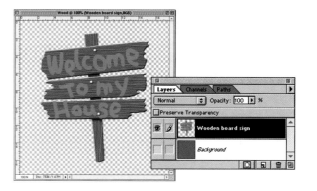

23

Create a new layer and move it below the 'Wooden Sign' layer. Name it 'Shadow.' Keep the 'Shadow' layer active, hold down the command (Ctrl) key and click on the 'Wooden Sign' layer on the Layers palette to load the selection. Choose Select > Feather and set the Feather Radius to 5 pixels. Fill the selection with black.

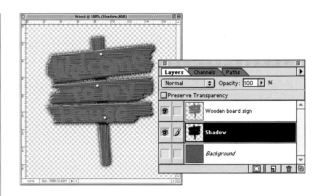

24

Deselect the selection. Choose Edit > Transform > Scale to reduce the height of the shadow. Use Edit > Transform > Distort to apply an angle to the shadow.

25

Choose Layer > Add Layer Mask > Reveal All. Leave the foreground color set to black and choose the Linear Gradient tool. Set the Gradient options to the diagram values and apply the gradient to the shadow from the top downward.

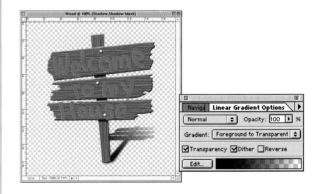

26

Create a new layer above the 'Wooden Sign' layer. Select the lower part of the post using the lasso tool and paint with the desired color. Fill the background layer with the same color and the image is complete.

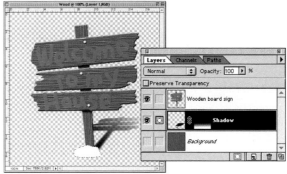

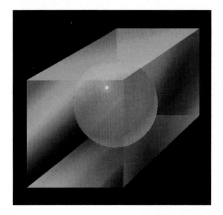

EXPRESSING TEXTURE WITH GRADIENTS

You can express qualitative differences in textures using gradient settings alone. By looking at the characteristics of various gradients, you should obtain a grasp of how to create textures.

1

Create a new file that is 500 x 500 pixels. Set the Resolution to 300 ppi and the Contents to White. Fill the background layer with black. Create a new layer named 'Sphere.' Choose the Elliptical Marquee tool and hold down the shift (Shift) key to draw a circle of any size.

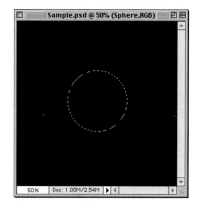

2

Choose the Radial Gradient tool and click Edit on the Gradient Tool Options palette to open the Gradient Editor. Click Load, and open Image > 1-06 > 'ball.grd' on the supplementary CD-ROM. Choose 'Plastic Red Ball' from the newly added gradient styles.

3

Set the Gradient options to the diagram values and fill the selection created in Step 1 with a gradient by dragging the cursor from the top left to the bottom right. The gradient for the plastic ball is characterized by few shading levels in comparison with metal, by highlights and deep shadows, and by a sharp reflection. You can increase the illusion of the plastic texture by drastically reducing the highlights.

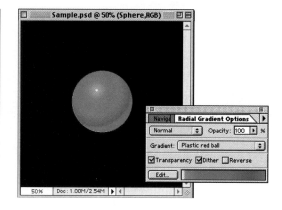

4

Next, we will create a glass cube. Although glass has abundant color variations, in this example we have prepared gradient styles that create translucent effects with any foreground color. Choose 'Glass Surface' from the pre-loaded gradient styles.

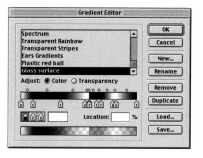

5

In the Gradient editor, set Adjust to Transparency. Define a multiple number of boxes as shown in the diagram. Select those boxes that are to be transparent and enter Opacity values. The lower the Opacity value, the greater the transparency.

6

Now, create a glass cube around the red ball. Create a new layer named 'Cube (Lower),' and move it below the 'Sphere' layer on the Layers palette. Set the foreground color to blue (R:86, G:222, B:222), then choose the Rectangular Marquee tool and hold down the shift (Shift) key to create a square selection behind the sphere. Choose the Linear Gradient tool, set the options to the diagram values and drag from the top left to the bottom right.

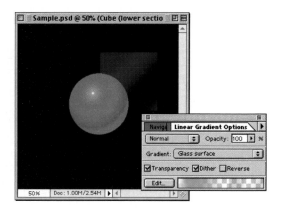

7

Duplicate the 'Cube (Lower)' layer. Choose Edit > Rotate 90° (Clockwise).

8

Move this part to the bottom edge of the first square with the Move tool. On the Layers palette, hold down the command (Ctrl) key and click on the 'Cube (Lower Part) Copy' layer to load its selection. The selection will not display if the pixel value is low. Use Edit > Free Transform and Edit > Transform > Distort to create the bottom face of the cube like that shown in the diagram. Merge this layer with the 'Cube (Lower)' layer.

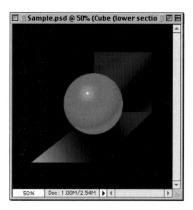

9

Create a new layer named 'Cube (Upper),' and move it above the 'Sphere' layer on the Layers palette. Create a selection for the front face of the cube of the same width as the 'Cube (Lower)' layer. Fill the selection with the 'Glass surface' gradient with the same procedures as you used on the lower part. Create the upper face of the cube repeating Steps 7 and 8.

10

For the remaining side, choose the Polygon Lasso tool to create a selection. Fill it with the 'Glass surface' gradient as before, dragging from the top left to the bottom right. The illustration is complete.

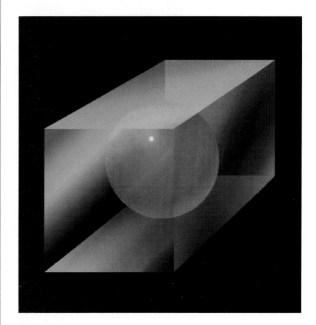

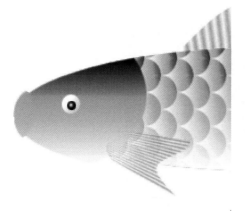

Chapter **1-7** *Carp*

CREATING DESIGNS WITH PATTERNS

It is easy to create patterns that make designs appear complex. The key is to make the patterns mesh well with each other.

1

Create a new file that is 30 x 30 pixels. Set the Resolution to 72 ppi and the Contents to White. Choose the Elliptical Marquee tool, set Style to Fixed Size and the Width and Height to 30 pixels. Draw a circular selection. Reset the foreground to its default color and select the Linear Gradient tool. Set the Gradient options to those in the diagram, and drag the cursor from right to left in the circle.

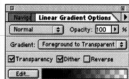

2

Duplicate the layer and set the blending mode to Multiply. Choose Filter > Others > Offset and set the values to those in the diagram. Apply the filter to complete the pattern for the fish scales. Select the entire image and choose Edit > Define Pattern to record the pattern. This file is also included on the supplementary CD-ROM as Images > 1-07 > scales.psd.

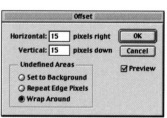

3

Create a new file that is 600 pixels wide and 300 pixels high and set the Contents to Transparent. Name the file 'Carp.' Change the name of 'Layer 1' to 'Body.' Choose the Elliptical Marquee tool, set the Style back to Normal and draw the oval selection that will become the carp's body. Choose Edit > Fill and set the Use list box to Pattern. Click OK.

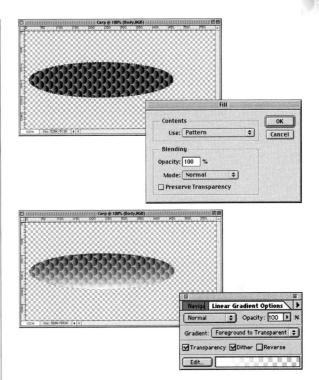

4

Change the foreground color to white. Choose the Linear Gradient tool. Set the options to the diagram values and the blending mode to Screen. Drag the cursor up from the bottom of the image to about the center of the oval.

5

Create a new layer named 'Head.' Select an area for the head with the Elliptical Marquee tool. Make the 'Body' layer active on the Layers palette, and choose Select > Load Selection. Set the Channel to 'Body Transparency' and the Operation to 'Intersect with Selection.' Click OK.

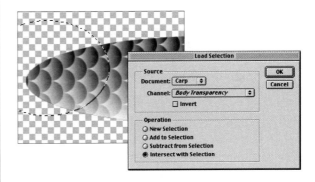

6

Reset the foreground and background to the default colors. Make the 'Head' layer active on the Layers palette. Choose the Linear Gradient tool, set the Gradient to 'Foreground to Background' and set the blending mode to Normal. Drag the cursor from the top of the screen to the bottom.

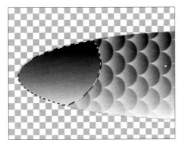

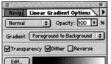

7

Choose Edit > Transform > Distort.
Drag the selection anchors to slightly enlarge
the Carp's head. Press the return (Enter) key
to accept the changes. Next, select the
vicinity of the Carp's mouth with the
Elliptical Marquee tool. Choose Filter >
Distort > Sphere and set the values to those
in the diagram. Click OK.

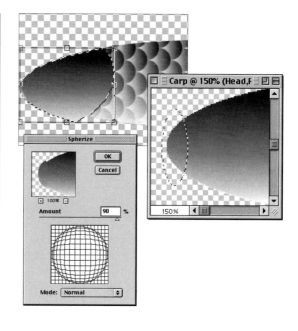

8

You will now make the fin patterns. Create a
new file that is 150 pixels wide and 10 pixels
high. Set the Contents to Transparent.
Choose the Linear Gradient tool with the
same settings as last time and drag the cursor
from top to bottom within the image.

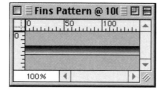

9

Select all, then choose Edit > Define Pattern
to record it as a pattern. Create a new file
named 'Fins' that is 150 x 150 pixels. Set the
Contents to Transparent. Choose Edit > Fill
and set Use to Pattern. Click OK. Choose
Filter > Stylize > Solarize. Click OK. Choose
Image > Adjust > Invert. This image is also
saved on the supplementary CD-ROM as
Images > 1-07 > fins.psd.

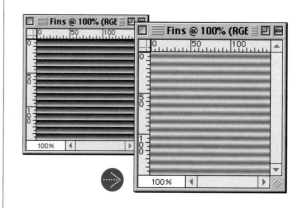

10

Select all, copy the contents and paste it onto the 'Carp' file. Choose Filter > Distort > Shear. Set the values to those in the diagram and click OK. Choose Edit > Transform > Distort to adapt the tail to the body. Name the layer 'Tail.'

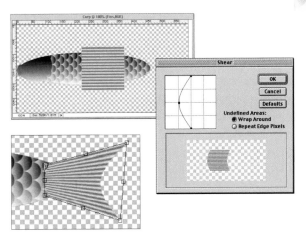

11

Create the breast, stomach and tail fins using the techniques in Step 10. Save each image on a separate layer.

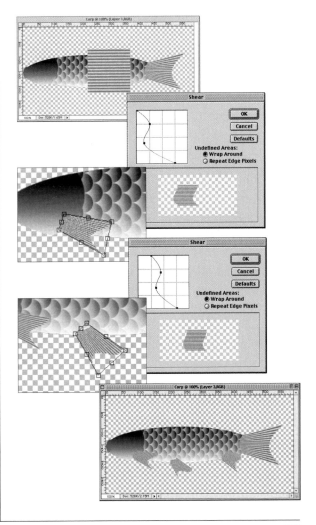

12

You will now create the dorsal fin. Use the same technique as for the other fins, but start from a file with a Width of 150 pixels and Height of 300 pixels. Follow the procedures in Step 9, then copy and paste the results into the Carp file. Next, choose Filter > Stylize > Shear. Modify it as shown in the diagram. Choose Edit > Transform > Rotate. Rotate the dorsal fin into position. You can further adjust its shape by choosing Edit > Transform > Distort.

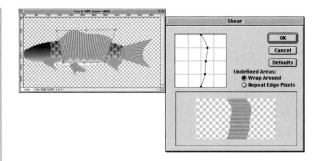

13

Set the opacity of each fin layer to 70%. Choose the Elliptical Marquee tool and select the areas where the 'Tail' and 'Breast' fins meet the body. Choose Select > Feather and set the Feather Radius to 5 pixels. Click OK. Deselect the selection. Move the 'Dorsal,' 'Stomach,' and 'Tail' fin layers below the 'Body' layer on the Layers palette.

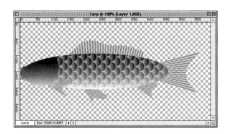

14

Now add color to the head and body. Make the 'Body' layer active. Choose Image > Adjust > Color Balance. Set the Shadows to (0, 0, 0), the Midtones to (+100, 0, 0) and the Highlights to (+100, -30, -50). Make the 'Head' layer active. Hold down the option (Alt) key and choose Image > Adjust > Color Balance to apply the command with same settings as the last time.

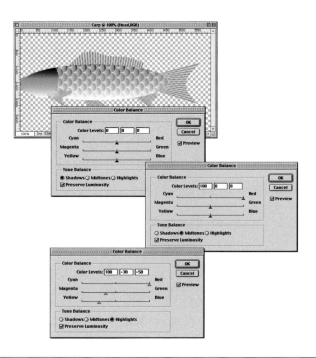

15

The last component is the eye. Create a new layer named 'Eye' above the 'Head' layer. Select the outline of the eye with the Elliptical Marquee tool. Change the foreground color to white. Choose the Linear Gradient tool and set it to the diagram values. Drag the cursor from the top left to the bottom right of the circle.

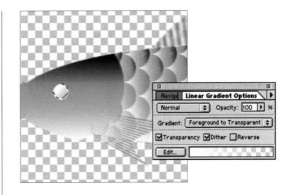

16

Select another smaller circle over the eye. Reset the foreground and background to the default colors and click the Switch color icon. Choose the Radial Gradient tool and set the values to those in the diagram. Drag the cursor from the top left to the bottom right of the circle. Your illustration is complete.

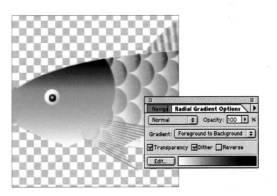

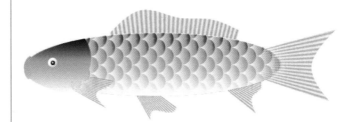

PRODUCING UNIQUE
APPEARANCES WITH FILTERS

Use filters to create the textures that are unique to computer graphics. Combine them with gradients to achieve rich 3-D effects.

1

Create a new file that is 500 x 500 pixels. Set the Resolution to 72 ppi and the Contents to Transparent. Choose the Rectangular Marquee tool to draw a selection that will become the television frame. Set the foreground color to yellow (R:254, G:188, B:11) and fill the selection.

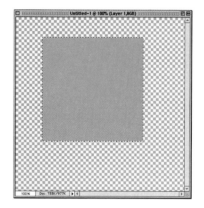

2

Select all and choose Edit > Cut, and Edit > Paste to paste the square in the center of the window. Rename 'Layer 1' to 'TV Frame.'

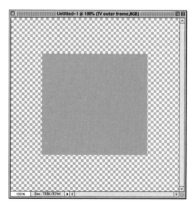

3

Choose Filter > Noise > Median, set the Radius to 10 pixels and click OK.

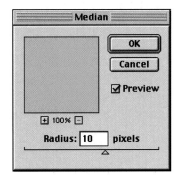

4

Create a new layer named 'Body.' Keep the 'Body' layer active and create a selection by holding down the command (Ctrl) key while you click on the 'TV Frame' layer. Choose Select > Modify > Contract and set the Contract By amount to 16 pixels. Click OK.

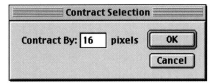

5

Choose Select > Feather, set the Feather Radius to 10 pixels and click OK. Fill the selection with the yellow used for the 'TV Frame.'

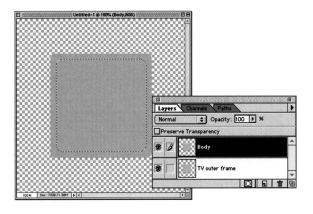

6

Create a new layer named 'Shadow' above the 'TV Frame' layer. Keep the 'Shadow' layer active, hold down the command (Ctrl) key and click on the 'TV Frame' layer on the Layers palette to load the selection. Reset the foreground and background to the default colors and click the Switch color icon. Choose the Linear Gradient tool and set the Gradient list box to 'Foreground to Background.' Drag from the top left to the bottom right of the selection. Set the Opacity of the 'Shadow' layer to 80%, and the blending mode to Hard Light.

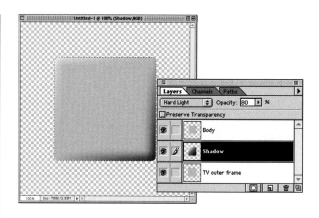

7

Choose Layer > Merge Visible to flatten the layers into one to be renamed 'TV.' Duplicate the 'TV' layer and name the copy 'Indent.' Choose Edit > Transform > Numeric and set the Scale Width and Height to 65%. Move the image slightly upward with the Move tool.

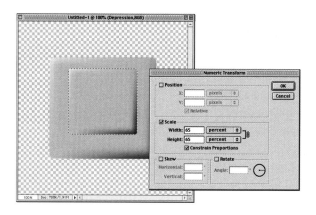

8

Choose Edit > Transform > Rotate 180° to rotate the 'Indent' layer.

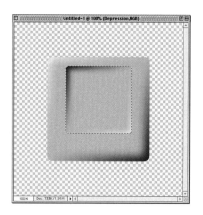

9

Create a new 'Monitor' layer above the 'Indent' layer on the Layers palette. Hold down the command (Ctrl) key and click on the 'Indent' layer to load the selection. Choose Select > Modify > Contract and set the Contract By amount to 3 pixels. Change the foreground color to white and the background to blue (R:5, G:0, B:210). Choose the Linear Gradient tool and set the values to those in the diagram. Drag the cursor from the top left to the bottom right in the selection.

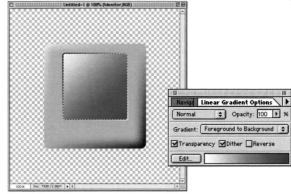

10

Create a new layer named 'Noise' above the 'Monitor' layer. Keep the Monitor selection active and fill it with white. Choose Filter > Noise > Add Noise. Set the Amount to 150, the Distribution to Uniform and click OK.

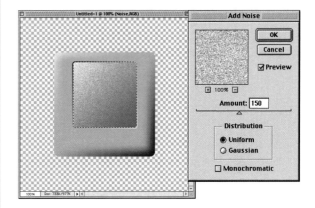

11

Change the Opacity of the 'Noise' layer to 50%. Choose Layer > Merge Visible to merge all the layers.

12

Deselect the selection. Choose Filter > Distort > Spherize. Set the Amount to 80% and the Mode to Normal.

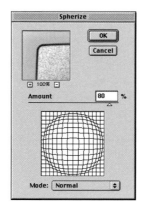

13

Create a new layer named 'Eyeball.' Hold the shift (Shift) key (to make it round) and draw a selection with the Elliptical Marquee tool to create the white of the eye. Set the foreground to white and the background to gray (R:97, G:97, B:97). Choose the Radial Gradient tool and set the Gradient to the value in the diagram. Drag the cursor from the top left to the bottom right of the selection.

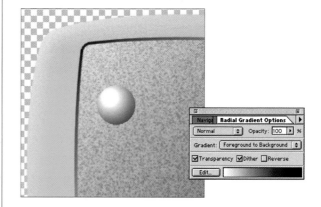

14

Create a layer named 'Pupil' above the 'Eyeball' layer. Draw over the white part of the eye to create the pupil selection. Change the foreground to light gray (R:191, G:191, B:191) and the background to black. Use the procedure in Step 13 to draw a gradient.

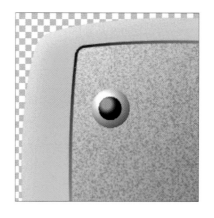

15

Hold down the command (Ctrl) key and click on the 'Eyeball' layer in the Layers palette to load the selection. Then hold down the option + shift (Alt + Shift) keys and move the eyeball to the right with the Move tool. This will duplicate the eyeball in the same layer. Use the Move tool to move the eyes into position.

16

Create a new layer named 'Mouth.' Draw a selection with the Elliptical Marquee tool to create the mouth. Fill it with white.

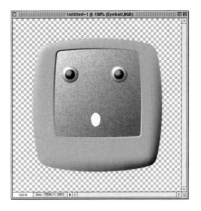

17

Create a new layer beneath 'Mouth.' Hold down the command (Ctrl) key and click on the 'Mouth' layer to load its selection. Choose Select > Modify > Expand and set the Expand Selection amount to 5 pixels. Choose Select > Feather and set the Feather Radius to 5 pixels. Reset the foreground and background to the default colors. Select the Linear Gradient tool and set the values to those in the diagram. Drag the cursor from the top left to the bottom right of the selection. Change the 'Layer 1' blending mode to Multiply. Merge all the layers and rename the result 'Face.'

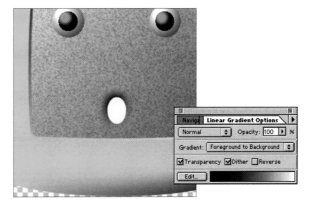

18

Create a new layer named 'Button' above the 'Face' layer. Choose the Elliptical Marquee tool, and hold down the shift (Shift) key while you draw a selection in the area you want to place a button. Switch the foreground and background colors. Choose the Radial Gradient tool. Drag from the top left to the bottom right to create a gradient.

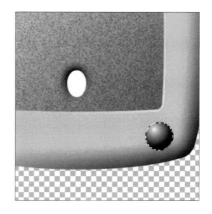

19

Draw a selection slightly smaller than the circle in Step 18 within the circle. Choose Select > Feather and set the Feather Radius to 3 pixels. Choose the Radial Gradient tool and drag from the bottom right to top left.

20

Create a new layer named 'Button 2' above the 'Button' layer. Draw a triangular selection with the Polygon Lasso tool as shown in the diagram. Fill it with gray (R:185, G:185, B:185).

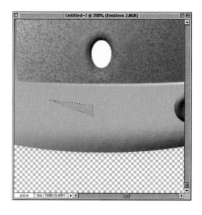

21

Select the lower area of the triangle with the Polygon Lasso tool. Choose Image> Adjust > Brightness/Contrast. Set the Brightness to -50 and click OK.

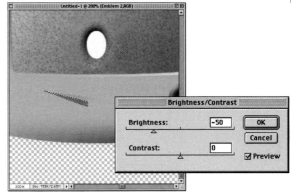

22

Choose Select > All. Copy the triangle by holding down the option + shift (Alt + Shift) keys and moving the triangle to the right with the Move tool. Choose Edit > Transform > Flip Horizontal. Move the new triangle up against the triangle on the left.

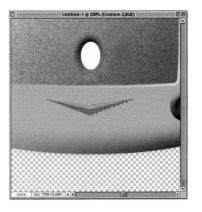

23

Keep the triangle selected and choose Image > Adjust> Brightness/Contrast. Set the Brightness to -50. Deselect the selection. Choose Select > All. Cut and paste the selection and adjust its position with the Move tool to complete the illustration.

ADDING LEGS

It's easy to give the television some legs by copying circles, transforming shapes and applying gradients.

1

Choose Layer > Merge Visible to flatten the television layers. Name the result 'Mr TV.' Create a new layer above it named 'Legs.' Choose the Elliptical Marquee tool. Hold down the shift (Shift) key and draw a circular selection. Fill the selection with blue (R:35, G:59, B:206). Hold down the command + option (Ctrl + Alt) keys and press the 'Up' cursor for an instant to stretch the circle.

2

Deselect the selection. Choose Edit > Transform > Perspective. Contract the lower part of the leg. Choose Edit > Transform > Rotate to tilt the leg to the right.

3

Duplicate the leg with the procedure in Step 22. Choose Edit > Transform > Flip Horizontal. Choose Select > All. Cut and paste to adjust the position. Shift the 'Legs' layer under the 'Mr TV' layer in the Layers palette. Change the foreground to black. Choose the Linear Gradient tool, set the values to those in the diagram and drag the cursor from the top to the bottom of each leg, one at a time, to complete the image.

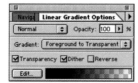

REPETITIONS USING ACTIONS

Repetitious procedures can be finished in a flash if the Actions feature is utilized to automate them. You can combine actions to significantly increase your efficiency.

1

Create a new file that is 200 x 200 pixels. Set the Resolution to 72 ppi and the Contents to Transparent. Choose the Elliptical Marquee tool and set the Style to Fixed Size, the Width to 40 pixels and the Height to 150 pixels. Click the image to create an oval selection. Fill the oval with light orange (R:222, G:156, B:107).

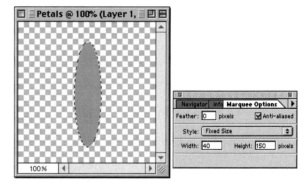

2

Choose New Action from the Actions palette menu. Name the action 'Petals' and click Record. Choose Layer > Duplicate Layer and set the blending mode to Exclusion. Choose Edit > Transform > Numeric and set the Scale Width to 80% and Height to 100%. Click the Stop button on the Actions palette to complete the recording of the 'Petals' action.

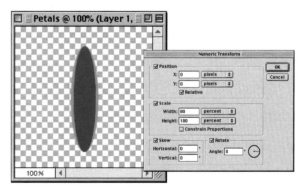

3

Choose 'Petals' on the Actions palette and play it five times. Deselect the selection. Since you have created 6 layers, choose Layer > Merge Visible to merge the layers.

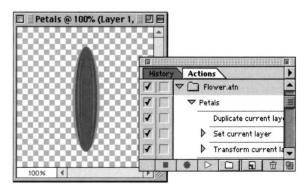

4

Choose Filter > Blur > Blur More. Click OK. Choose Filter > Stylize> Solarize. Click OK. Choose Image > Adjust> Invert to change the colors.

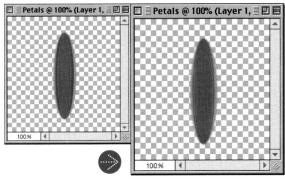

5

Choose Select > All to select the entire Petals image. Copy it, create a new file named 'Flower' that is 42 x 152 pixels, and paste the petal into it. Choose Image > Canvas Size and set the values to those in the diagram.

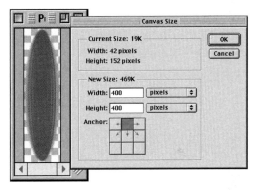

6

Hold down the command (Ctrl) key and click 'Layer 1' in the Layers palette to load the petal selection. Choose Select > Inverse.
Fill the selection with white. Choose Select > Inverse to reverse the selection again. Choose Layer > Add Layer Mask > Reveal Selection.

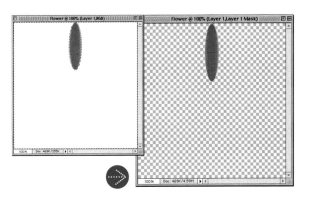

7

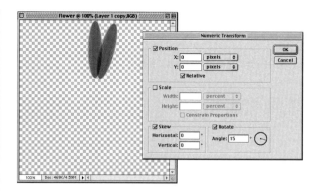

Choose New Action from the Actions palette menu. Name the action 'Flower' and click Record. Duplicate the layer and set the blending mode to Multiply. Choose Edit > Transform > Numeric. Remove the check from the Scale checkbox and set the Rotation angle to 15°. Click the Stop button on the Actions palette to complete the recording of the 'Flower' action.

8

Choose the 'Flower' action and play it four times. Choose Layer > Merge Visible.

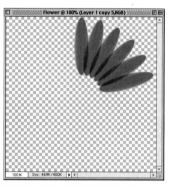

9

Choose Select > Load Selection, set the Channel to 'Layer 1 Copy 5 Transparency' and place a check in the Invert checkbox. Fill the selection with white. Choose Selection > Inverse. Choose Layer > Add Layer Mask > Reveal Selection.

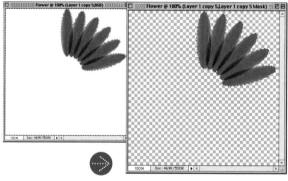

10

Choose New Action from the Action palette menu. Name the action 'Flower 90 Degrees' and click Record. Duplicate the layer and set the blending mode to Multiply. Choose Edit > Transform > Numeric and set the Rotation to 15°. Click the Stop button on the Actions palette to complete the recording of the 'Flower 90 Degrees' action.

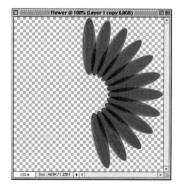

11

Choose the 'Flower 90 Degrees' action and play it twice. Choose Layer > Merge Visible to merge the layers and name the results 'Flower.'

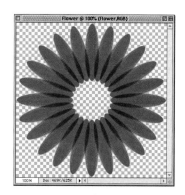

12

Choose Image > Adjust > Invert.

13

Choose Image > Adjust > Hue/Saturation and set the Hue to 30. Choose Image > Adjust > Color Balance and set the shadows and highlights to the values in the diagrams.

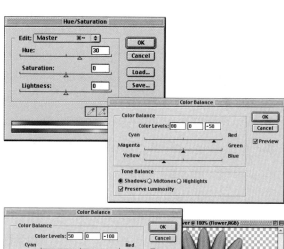

14

Create a new 'Pistil' layer beneath the 'Flower' layer on the Layers palette. Choose the Elliptical Marquee tool and set the Style to Fixed Size and the Width and Height to 150 pixels. Select the center of the flower. Choose the Radial Gradient tool and set the values to those in the diagram. Set the foreground color to orange (R:200, G:107, B:0) and the background to brown (R:93, G:50, B:0). Drag from the top left to the bottom right of the selection.

15

Choose Filter > Noise > Add Noise. Set the Amount to 100 and the Distribution to Uniform. Click OK.

16

Choose Filter > Stylize > Solarize. Click OK. Choose Image > Adjust > Invert. Click OK. Choose Image > Adjust > Hue/Saturation and set the values to those in the diagram.

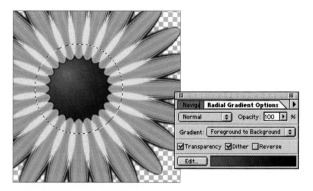

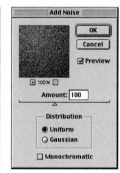

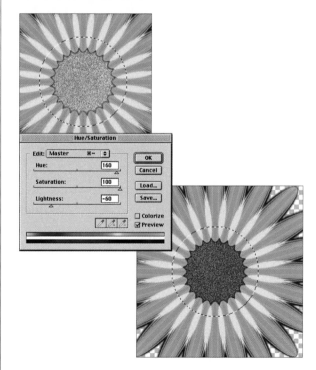

17

Keep the center of the flower selected and make the 'Flower' layer active. Place a check in the Preserve Transparency checkbox. Choose Select > Feather and set the Feather Radius to 15 pixels. Reset the foreground and background to the default colors. Choose Edit > Fill, and set Use to 'Foreground Color' and the Blending Mode to Multiply. Fill the selection to complete the image.

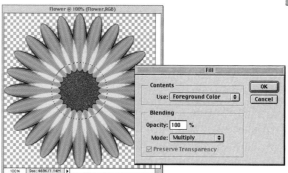

TIPS

The Action files created and used in this manual are included on the CD-ROM. To load these files, choose Load Actions from the Actions palette menu and open Images > 1-09 > flower.atn.

MAKING RANDOM PATTERNS

Try your hand at making seamless random patterns. They can be printed to create wrapping paper and other items, or used for backgrounds for web sites and graphic art.

1

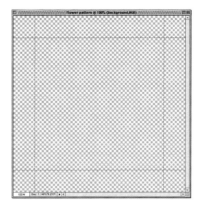

Create a new file that is slightly larger than the pattern you wish to create. In this case, we have created 'Flower Pattern,' a 630 x 630 pixel (8 x 8 cm) file with the Resolution set to 200 ppi. Pull out guides from the rulers and place them inside the image as shown in the diagram so that they form a 6 x 6 cm square, the size of the finished pattern. Choose View > Snap to Guides and place a check beside this item.

2

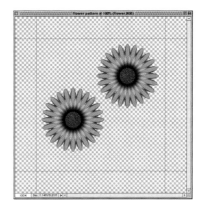

Create a new layer. Copy and paste the image from the 'Flower' file into the new layer.

3

Create several layers containing copies of the flower. Make variations using the Image > Adjust > Hue/Saturation and Layer > Transform > Scale command to change the colors and sizes. Ensure that the flowers do not extend beyond the outside image borders and that no two flowers overlap on the same layer.

4

Display a portion of the image perimeter so that it is easy to select. Choose the Rectangular Marquee tool and select the square at the top left-hand corner outside the guides. Activate the layer that contains this image.

5

Choose the Move tool. Cut and paste the selection by dragging it to the guides at the diametrically opposed corner at the bottom right of the image. It should touch both guides.

6

Use the same procedure to select the area outside the left guide. Hold down the shift (Shift) key while you move the selection over to the inside of the right guide.

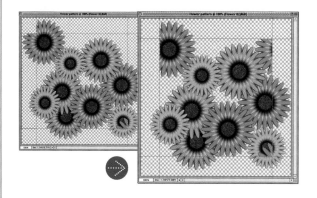

7

Since part of a small yellow flower still remains, you must activate the layer that includes this flower and repeat the procedure.

8

Use these procedures to select all portions that extend past the guides and to cut and paste them inside the opposite guides on all layers.

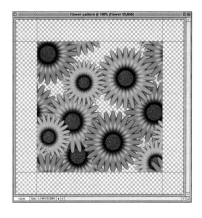

TIPS

The reason this operation must be repeated for individual layers is to avoid changing the way the flowers overlap. Although it is time-consuming, it is better to process each layer individually.

9

The next step is to color the background. We used a light brown (R:179, G:51, B:16) in this example. Choose Filter > Noise > Add Noise with the settings indicated in the diagram to alter the texture.

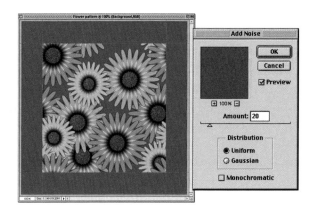

10

Flatten the layers. Crop the image along the guides. Choose Select > All. Choose Edit > Define Pattern. The flower pattern has now been recorded as a pattern.

TIPS

This Pattern is contained on the supplementary CD-ROM. Open Images > 1-09 > flowerpattern.psd.

11

Create a new file and fill it with this pattern. Choose Edit > Fill and set the values to those in the diagram. This will fill the image with the flower pattern.

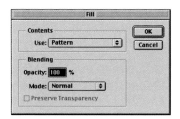

REALISTIC GROOVES CREATED WITH FILTERS

Difficult-looking textures are easy with filters. By simply changing settings, a variety of appearances - not only the grooves on a record -can be expressed.

1

Create a new file that is 500 x 500 pixels. Set the Resolution to 72 ppi and the Contents to Transparent. Rename Layer 1'Grooves.' Select all, change the foreground to white and fill with white. Choose Filter > Noise > Add Noise. Set the Amount to 999, the Distribution to Uniform, and place a check in the Grayscale checkbox.

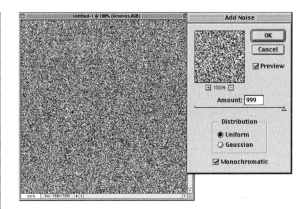

2

Choose Filter > Blur > Radial Blur and set the Amount to 100, the Blur Method to Spin and the Quality to Good. Repeat the effect once by pressing the command + F (Ctrl + F) keys.

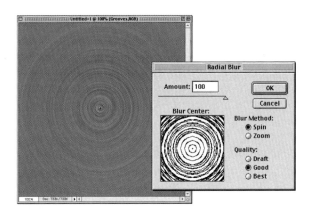

3

Create a new layer named 'Shape.' Choose the Elliptical Marquee tool. Hold down the shift (Shift) key and drag the cursor from the corner toward the center of the screen, selecting a large circle in the process. Fill the circle with black. Deselect the selection. Select all, choose Edit > Cut and Edit > Paste. This will center the black circle. Set the Opacity of the layer to 80% in the Layers palette.

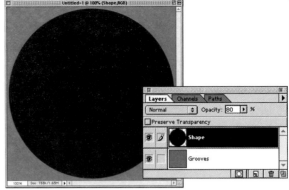

4

Make the 'Groove' layer active. Hold down the command (Ctrl) key and click the 'Shape' layer in the Layers palette to load its selection. Keep the selection active and choose Layer > Add Layer Mask > Reveal Selection. Click the thumbnail on the 'Groove' layer in the Layers palette.

5

Duplicate the 'Groove' layer with the Layers palette menu and rename the result 'Light.' Shift the 'Light' layer above the 'Shape' layer. Use the Polygon Lasso tool to make a cross-over selection like the one in the diagram. Choose Select > Feather and set the Feather Radius to 20 pixels.

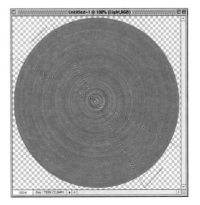

6

Keep the 'Light' layer selected and choose Select > Inverse then delete the selection with the delete (Backspace) key. Deselect the selection.

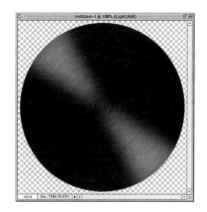

7

Merge the layers into one using Layer > Merge Visible and rename the result 'Record.' Choose Image > Adjust > Brightness/Contrast. Set the Contrast to +55 and click OK.

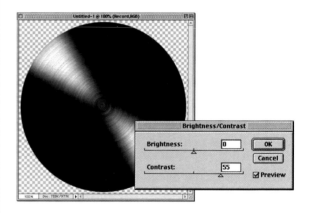

8

Choose Filter > Blur > Radial Blur and set the values to those in the diagram. Create a new layer named 'Label.' Choose the Elliptical Marquee tool, hold down the option + shift (Alt + Shift) keys and drag a perfect circle to size, starting from the record's center and extending part way to the bottom right corner. Fill the selection with yellow (R:255, G:204, B:0). Deselect the selection.

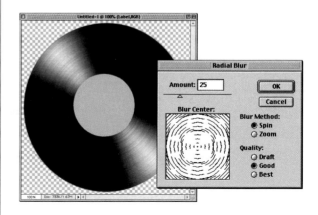

9

Create a new layer, 'Layer 1,' above the 'Record' layer and make it active. Hold down the command (Ctrl) key while you click on the 'Label' layer to load its selection. Choose Select > Modify > Expand and set the Expand By amount to 10 pixels. Click OK. Fill the selection with black.

10

Hold down the command (Ctrl) key and click on the 'Record' layer to load its selection. Change the foreground color to black. Choose Edit > Stroke and set the Stroke Width to 8 pixels and the Location to Center. Click OK.

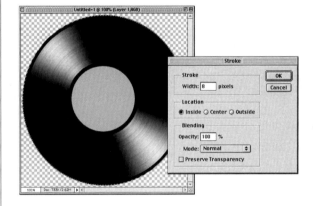

11

Hide the 'Label' layer and 'Layer 1' to display the center portion of the disk. Use the Elliptical Marquee tool to draw a perfect circular selection using the procedure in Step 8, dragging outward from the center of the disk to an appropriate spot.

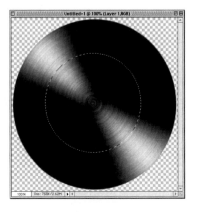

12

Show the hidden 'Layer 1.' Choose Edit > Stroke and set the Stroke Width to 3 pixels and the Location to Center. Click OK.

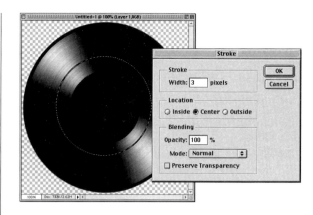

13

Repeat Step 12 to create another 3 pixel line at an appropriate spacing to mimic the grooves between songs. Show the 'Label' layer again, link the three layers to the 'Record' layer, and merge them all together.

14

Create a new layer (Layer 1). Draw a small circle by holding down the shift (Shift) key and dragging the Elliptical Marquee tool. Fill the circle with black. Cut and paste the selection to center it. Make the 'Record' layer active. Hold down the command (Ctrl) key and click on 'Layer 1.' Delete with the delete (Backspace) key.

15

Return to 'Layer 1.' Choose Select > Feather and set the Feather Radius to 2 pixels. Click OK. Shift 'Layer 1' below the 'Record' layer, and shift the selection about 3 pixels down with the cursor key on the keyboard. Delete the selection with the delete (Backspace) key to complete the image.

3-D WITH GRADIENTS

Although coloring illustrations so they retain three-dimensional appearances traditionally involved considerable effort, Photoshop makes it easy with gradients.

1

Start by preparing the file with the line drawing on which the illustration is based. You can also create a new file and use the Line and Paintbrush tools to sketch your own line drawing. If you do, ensure that every part forms an enclosure so that it can be individually selected. Open Image > 1-11 > 'robot.psd' on the supplementary CD-ROM. Duplicate the 'Background' layer, naming the result 'Selection.'

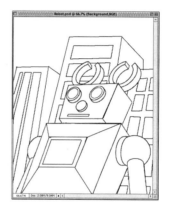

2

Select a surface (enclosure) with the Magic Wand tool. Choose Edit > Stroke and set the Location to Outside and select a Stroke Width that covers the sketch lines adequately. We have used 3 pixels in this example. Select easily distinguished colors at this point because the final colors will be selected later. If a line is severed somewhere and the surface can't be easily selected, use the Pencil tool to fix it.

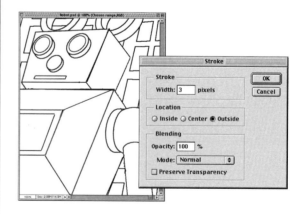

3

Choose the Paint Bucket tool, set the Tolerance to 1 and deselect the Anti-alias checkbox. Fill in the selection with the color you used to stroke the outline in Step 2. The outlines and interior of the windows, robot eyes and other parts not in direct contact with other sections can be easily filled by clicking them with the Paint Bucket tool.

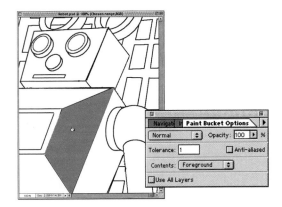

4

Change the foreground color each time and perform the same procedures on all the other surfaces, giving each a different color to its neighbor. Close up any gaps with the Line or Pencil tools.

5

You will now use gradients with a metallic texture and others with a spherical texture on the robot's surfaces. Choose the Linear Gradient tool and click the Edit button on the Gradient Tool Options palette to open the Gradient Editor. Click the Load button to open Images > 1-11 > 'robot.grd.' Select 'Stainless Surface' from the list box. Since you will add colors later on, you can create the gradients in gray at present as shown in the diagram.

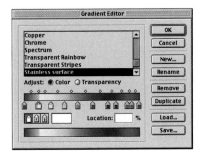

6

Create a new layer named 'Color Fill' above the 'Selection' layer. Make the 'Selection' layer active. Choose the Magic Wand tool, set the Tolerance to 1 and deselect the Anti-alias checkbox.

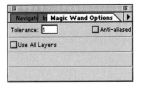

7

Select a surface you wish to paint, choose Select > Similar, and select the areas that could not be selected with the Magic Wand tool. Make the 'Color Fill' layer active. Choose the Linear Gradient tool and set the Gradient to Stainless Surface. Drag the cursor as you wish to apply a gradient.

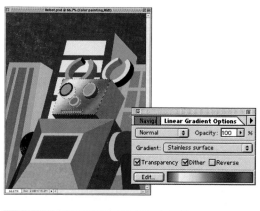

8

For spherical areas such as the joint between the robot's arm and body, select the Radial Gradient tool and set the Gradient option to 'Stainless Sphere.' Since a reflection will be applied later to the 'Stainless Sphere' areas, you should start the gradient with white on the left edge. Do this by dragging the cursor from the top left to the bottom right within all circular selections.

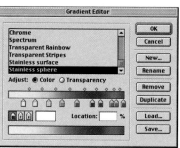

9

Set the foreground color to a light gray (R:64, G:64, B:64) and the background color to white to apply gradients to the walls of the building and the sky. Choose the Linear Gradient tool and set the Gradient option to 'Foreground to Background.' The appearance of the resulting gradient will vary substantially according to how far, and at what angle, you drag the cursor. Try several different combinations of stroke length and angle, until you achieve satisfactory results. Keep in mind that light will be shining on the object from the upper left. You can make the entire image more consistent by applying the gradient down from the upper left.

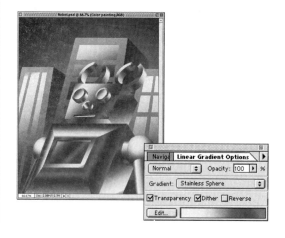

10

Although you have given parts of the robot a metallic appearance, the image as a whole lacks shadows. To add shadows, you will select areas with the Magic Wand tool on the 'Selection' layer for shading. Make the 'Color Fill' layer active. Choose Image > Adjust > Brightness/Contrast and set the Brightness to the value in the diagram to reduce the brightness. Select the areas that are to be even darker and set the Brightness to -50 and Contrast to -30.

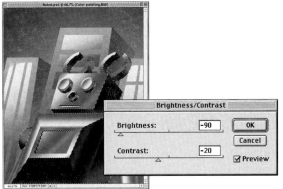

11

The last step is to apply the final colors. Create a new layer named 'Color' at the very top of the Layers palette. Set the blending mode to Color. Make the 'Selection' layer active and select the various areas with the Magic Wand tool to apply the colors. Areas to be filled with the same colors can be simultaneously selected by holding down the shift (Shift) key while clicking them. Make the 'Color' layer active and choose Edit > Fill. Set the Contents Use option to Foreground Color and the Blending option to Color. Fill the various areas to complete the illustration.

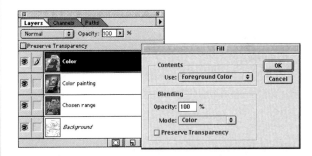

DRAWING PATTERNS WITH THE LINE TOOL

Try your hand at sketching national flags and illustrations with the Line tool. The Line tool can also be used to draw rectangles in a single step.

1

Create a new file that is 500 x 500 pixels. Set the Resolution to 72 ppi and Contents to Transparent. Set the foreground color to red (R:255, G:0, B:0). Choose the Line tool and set the blending mode to Normal, Opacity to 100% and the Line Width to 50 pixels. Hold down the shift (Shift) key and draw a horizontal line.

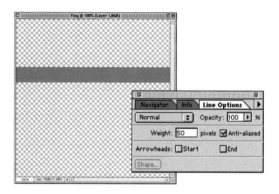

2

To center this line, choose Select > All, then Edit > Cut and Edit > Paste.

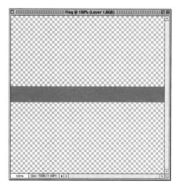

3

Create a new layer. Repeat Steps 1 and 2 on this layer, but draw the line vertically this time. Use the cut and paste commands to center the line in the image.

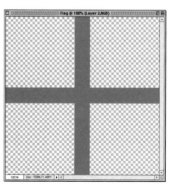

4

Choose Layer > Merge Down to combine the layers. Rename the resulting layer 'Lines.' Create a new layer (Layer 1) and move it under the 'Lines' layer.

5

Draw a selection with the Rectangular Marquee tool in the shape of the flag. Change the foreground color to blue (R:0, G:0, B:255) and fill the rectangle. Use the procedure in Step 2 to center the blue rectangle in the image by cutting and pasting. Create a new layer (Layer 2) above 'Layer 1.'

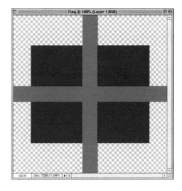

6

Keep 'Layer 2' selected, hold down the command (Ctrl) key and click on the 'Lines' layer to load its selection into Layer 2.

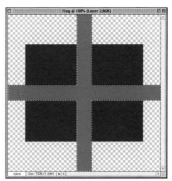

7

Choose Select > Modify > Expand and set the Expand By option to 10 pixels and click OK.

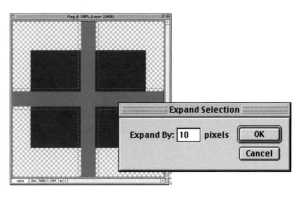

8

Set the foreground color to white and fill the selection. Merge the 'Layer 2' and 'Lines' layers and name the result 'Lines.' Create a new layer and place it beneath the 'Lines' layer.

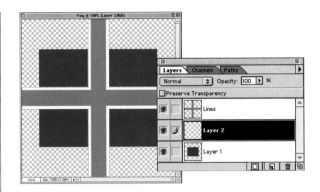

9

Use the Eyedropper tool to set the foreground color to red. Choose the Line tool and set it to the same values as in Step 2. Align the cross-pointer over the top left corner of the flag and drag it to the bottom right corner. Do the same from the top right corner down to the bottom left.

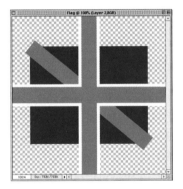

10

Create a new layer below 'Layer 2,' and draw white trim lines along the red lines using the techniques in Steps 7 and 8.

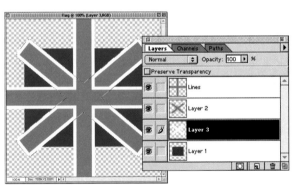

11

Combine all the layers except 'Layer 1.' Keep the combined layer active and hold down the command (Ctrl) key and click on 'Layer 1' to load its selection. Choose Select > Inverse to reverse the selection. Delete the portions of the stripes extruding beyond the flag by clicking on the delete (Backspace) key. Merge all the layers and name the result 'Union Jack.'

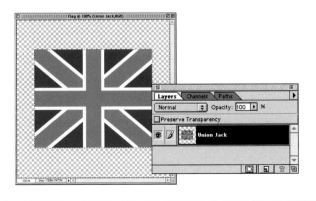

12

Create a new layer. Draw a selection with the Rectangular Marquee tool to serve as the flag pole. Reset the foreground and background to the default colors and switch them. Choose the Linear Gradient tool and set the values to those in the diagram. Drag from left to right in the selection.

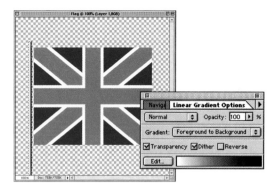

13

Draw a small circle with the Elliptical Marquee tool at the tip of the pole. Set the foreground color to yellow (R:244, G:241, B:0) and the background to black. Choose the Radial Gradient tool and drag the cursor from the top left to the bottom right of the selection to apply a 3-D effect.

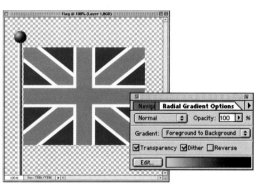

14

Select the 'Union Jack' layer and choose Filter > Distort > Twirl. Set the Angle to 40 degrees and apply the filter.

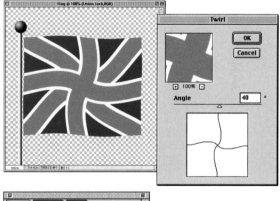

15

Create a new layer right above the 'Union Jack' layer. Hold down the command (Ctrl) key and click on the 'Union Jack' layer to load its selection. Choose Layer > Add Layer Mask > Reveal Selection. Make 'Layer 2' active by clicking its thumbnail.

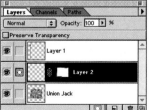

16

Change the foreground color to white and the background color to black. Choose the Linear Gradient tool and drag from about a quarter of the way in from the left side of the flag to its center. Change the Gradient option to Foreground to Transparent and drag from about a quarter of the way in from the right side of the flag to its center.

17

Set the 'Layer 2' blending mode to Multiply and Opacity to 60% to finish the illustration.

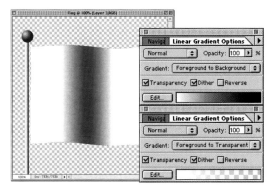

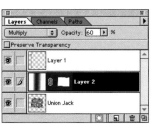

Chapter ①

SUMMER GREETING CARDS

Draw a background that fits in with the illustration to create a nice
cool image. Use coated paper stock to print postcards.

Chapter ①

MOUSE PADS/FLOPPY DISK LABELS

You can create your own mouse pad design using kits available on the market. Print floppy disk labels on adhesive labels that are approved for your printer.

STATIONERY SETS

Use your original illustrations to create your own stationery.

Craft your own envelopes from the images you print out.

Add a patterned liner to your envelopes or print patterns on the back of your letterhead to demonstrate your creativity.

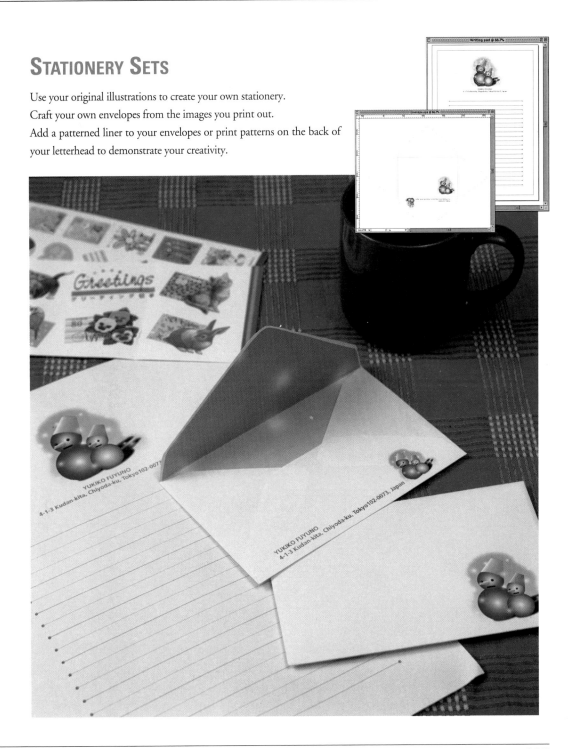

Chapter ①

WRAPPING PAPER

Print a random pattern on a large sheet to make original wrapping paper.

You can put this technique to countless uses, ranging from small present bags to bookmarks and book covers.

PHOTO EDITING

Although photo editing is widely accepted to be Photoshop's primary forte, use of the program is often limited to altering the brightness and coloring of images captured with digital cameras. This may be said to be creativity at a certain level, but this chapter will show you how to achieve works of greater originality.

In this chapter, we introduce you to techniques that use digital images simply as raw materials for entirely new works of art. Learn from professionals how to apply and combine filters, create collages from close-cropped images and process images with a sense of style. You will also learn numerous tricks for generating original characters and illustrations.

Needless to say, you can achieve all this without having to learn particularly difficult techniques. To create original artwork based on your own images, all you need to do is understand the basics of each exercise.

Amusing Collages

Create an amusing picture by assembling elements of different photos. The key is to copy and paste so that the images appear natural.

1

Open the image you want to crop. For this step, open Images > 2-01 > Material > dog.psd on the supplementary CD-ROM. Click the Quick Mask mode icon on the toolbox to enter the Quick Mask mode. Start by choosing one of the larger Paintbrush tools to paint the surrounding area, being careful not to approach too close to the dog's face at first.

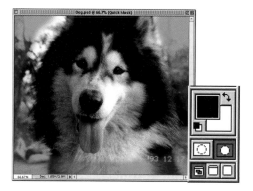

2

Choose the Airbrush tool and select the 3 pixel brush (Double-click a brush in the Brushes palette to see its specs). Set the options to the diagram values and carefully select the background image following the flow of the dog's fur. If you are having trouble selecting the dog's face, please note that this selection has already been saved as an alpha channel 1 in the Channels palette. You can load it by opening the Channels palette, holding down the command (Ctrl) key and clicking on it. Copy and paste the selection, naming the new layer 'Dog's Face.'

3

Open the second source file. Open Images > 2-01 > Material > dog2.psd on the supplementary CD-ROM. Copy the area around the left eye with the Rectangular Marquee tool and paste it onto the 'dog.psd' file. Name the layer 'Wink.' Position the new selection over the original image.

4

To match the color tones, choose Images > Adjust > Levels, and watch the image on your monitor as you adjust. Choose Images > Adjust > Color Balance to further refine the selection.

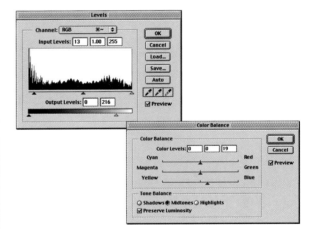

5

Choose the Lasso tool and select the approximate area of the face. Choose Select > Inverse to reverse the selection. Delete the unneeded portion of the image with the delete [Backspace] key. Drag the Smudge tool around the edges of the image, changing the size and pressure to suit the area. Choose a pressure of 75% for thin lines and 45% for thick lines.

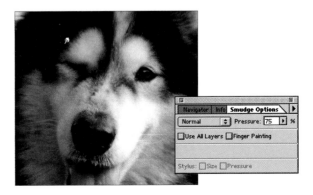

6

Open the third source image. Open Images >
2-01 > Material > frame.psd on the supplementary CD-ROM. Select the frame of the
eyeglasses using the Quick Mask mode and
the Airbrush tool. An alpha channel 1 is also
available for this file. Follow the procedure in
Step 2 if you wish to load the prepared selection from the Channels palette. Copy the
selection, paste it onto the 'dog.psd' file and
name the layer 'Glasses.' Choose Edit >
Transform > Rotate to tilt the glasses to a
position that appears natural.

7

Open the fourth source file. Open Images > 2-
01 > Material > shirt.psd on the supplementary
CD-ROM. Select only the clothing portion
using the procedure you used on the glasses.
An alpha channel 1 is also available for this file.
Follow the procedure in Step 2 if you wish to
load the prepared selection from the Channels
palette. Copy the selection and paste it onto
the 'dog.psd' file, naming the layer 'Shirt.'
Since the clothing appears small in proportion
to the dog's face, choose Edit > Transform >
Scale to stretch the clothing. Choose the Eraser
tool to erase the area of the 'Shirt' layer where
it overlaps the 'Dog's face.'

8

Apply a shadow from the top right to the
lower left of the shirt to make the intersection
of the face and clothing appear natural.
Choose the Lasso tool and select the area for
the shadow. Choose Select > Feather and set
the Feather Radius to 60 pixels. Choose
Images > Adjust > Levels, set the options to
the diagram values and adjust as required.

9

Make the 'Background' layer active. Choose the Rectangular Marquee tool and select the red and green area with the flowers on the right-hand side. Copy and paste the selection. Choose Edit > Transform > Scale on the new layer to expand the selection to fill the full background. Choose Layer > Flatten Image to combine all the layers.

10

Choose Filter > Noise > Add Noise and set the options to the diagram values. Click OK to complete the image.

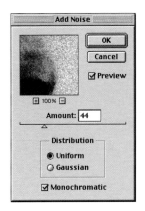

ADAPTING PHOTOS TO ILLUSTRATIONS

Try using Photoshop's outstanding capabilities to create surrealistic scenes. Transform ordinary photographs by adding an illustrated character.

1

Open the source files for the exercise. First select the background image. Open Images > 2-02 > build.psd on the supplementary CD-ROM. Next, open Images > 2-02 > chara.psd on the supplementary CD-ROM. Make the 'Character' layer active. Choose Select > All and copy and paste the selection into the 'build.psd' file. Name the new layer 'Character.' Move the image slightly upward.

2

Hide the 'Character' layer. Make the 'Background' layer active and duplicate it, naming this layer 'Sky.' Keep the 'Sky' layer active and open the Channels palette. Hold down the command (Ctrl) key and click the 'Building' channel to load the selection of the area above the rooftops. Choose Edit > Transform > Scale and expand the selection to the bottom of the window. Now move the image slightly upward as shown.

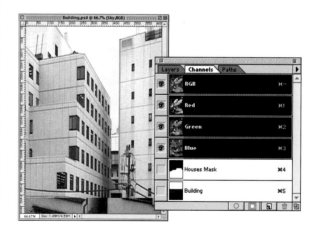

3

Make the 'Background' layer active and open the Channels palette. Hold down the command (Ctrl) key and click the 'Houses mask' to select the area with the houses. Copy and paste the selection, naming the new layer 'Houses.' Move the 'Houses' layer above the 'Sky' layer in the Layers palette.

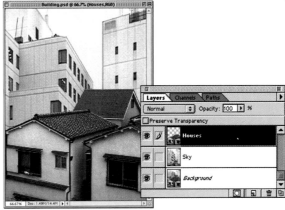

4

Show the 'Character' layer and move the 'Houses' layer slightly downward to avoid overlapping the character.

5

Make the 'Sky' layer active and choose Images > Adjust > Invert to transform it into a night scene.

6

Choose Images > Adjust > Brightness/
Contrast. Set the Brightness to 45 and the
Contrast to 25. Choose Images > Adjust > Hue
/Saturation and set the Saturation to -100.

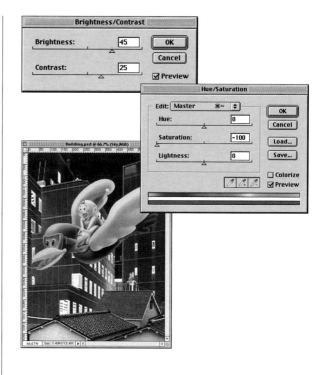

7

Choose Filter > Noise > Median and set the
Radius to 7 pixels. Choose Filter > Blur >
Gaussian Blur and set the Radius to 7 pixels.

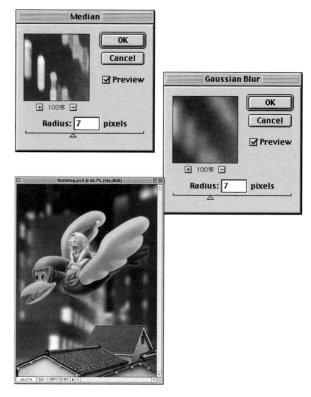

8

Similarly, choose Images > Adjust > Invert for the 'House' layer. Choose Images > Adjust > Hue/Saturation and set the Saturation to -100. Choose Filter > Noise > Median and set the Radius to 4 pixels. Choose Filter > Blur > Gaussian Blur and set the Radius to 3 pixels.

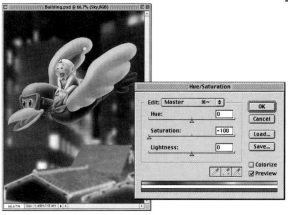

9

Finally, create a new layer beneath the 'Character' layer named 'Color.' Change the layer's blending mode to Color. Choose the Airbrush tool, select a large brush and add colors to portions of the image to match the color scheme of the illustration to complete the exercise.

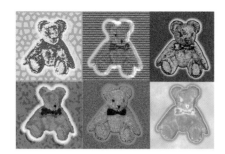

POP ART WITH FILTERS

Create an Andy Warhol style 'pop art' postcard with a close-cropped image from a photograph. A vast array of variations can be created by applying filters in different ways.

1

Start by creating a new file with the dimensions of a postcard. Create a new file with dimensions of 10 x 15 cm. Set the resolution to 300 ppi and the Contents to White. Choose View > Show Grid. Choose View > Show Rulers. Choose View > Snap to Grid. Pull out two vertical and one horizontal guide to divide the image into six equal squares.

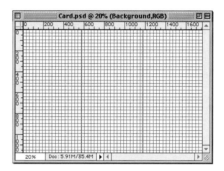

2

Choose the Rectangular Marquee tool. Select squares within the areas defined by the guides. Choose the Paint Bucket tool and fill each square with a different color. Make sure that the colors of adjacent squares are not similar.

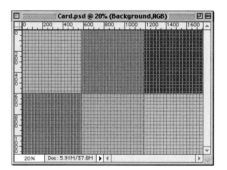

3

You will now apply effects to the background with filters using the diagram settings. The settings are for a 300 dpi image. If you are working with the low-resolution images, you should adjust each setting to a lower value. Please note that the completed backgrounds are also available on the supplementary CD-ROM if you choose Images > 2-03 > back_300.psd or back_150.psd. Choose the Magic Wand to select each square in turn. Choose Filter > Texture > Stained Glass and apply it to the upper left square. Choose Filter > Texture > Texturizer and apply it to the upper middle square. Choose Filter > Noise > Add Noise and apply it to the upper right and lower middle squares. Choose Filter > Artistic > Sponge and apply it to the lower left square. Choose Filter > Render > Clouds and apply it to the lower right square.

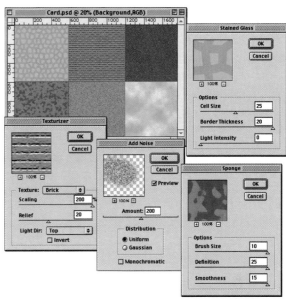

4

Open the files with the images you will close-crop. Images without fragmented edges and a relatively uncluttered background are best for this. For this exercise, open the supplementary CD-ROM and choose Images > 2-03 > bear_300.psd or bear_150.psd.' Duplicate the 'Background' layer. Change the foreground color to white, choose the Paintbrush tool and paint around the bear with one of the larger brushes. Carefully fill in the fine areas around the bear's outline with a small brush.

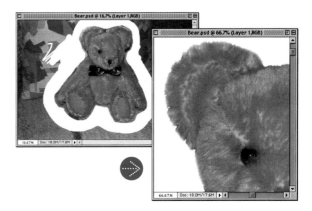

5

If the outline is too jagged, the end result will look too much like a cut and paste job. To avoid this, blur the edges of the more distinct areas with a large brush. Choose the Rubber Stamp tool to remove any scratches or smears from the image.

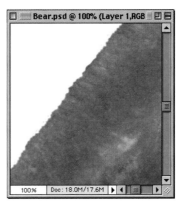

6

After you have painted the area surrounding the bear, choose the Lasso or Rectangular Marquee tool to select the bear and part of the white border. Copy and paste the selection. Choose the Magic Wand tool to select the white area. Press the delete (Backspace) key to delete it, making the area around the bear transparent. When you have isolated the bear, copy it. Save the initial file if necessary. Please note that the image of the close-cropped bear is also available on the supplementary CD-ROM if you choose Images > Materials > 2-03> bear2.psd.

7

Paste the close-cropped bear image onto the upper left corner of the 'Background' layer and name the new layer 'Bear 1.' If your image does not fit the square, scale it as required. The bear in this exercise is reduced to 50%. Duplicate the 'Bear 1' layer five times to create layers numbered 'Bear 2' through 'Bear 6.' Align the photographs in order from left to right, top to bottom. Since Snap to Grid was chosen in Step 1, positioning images is easy because they stick to the grid lines.

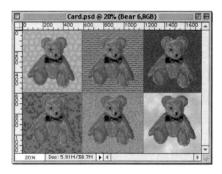

8

We will now apply different processing to each of the bear layers. First, duplicate the 'Bear 1' layer to superimpose one bear on top of the other. Make the original 'Bear 1' layer active and choose Filter > Texture > Texturizer and set the options to the diagram values. Set the layer's blending mode to Color Dodge and Opacity to 32%. Make the 'Bear 1 copy' layer active and set the foreground color to brown (R:159, G:121, B:57) and the background to white. Choose Filter > Sketch > Note Paper and set the options to the diagram values. Make the 'Bear 1' layer active, choose the Move tool and shift it slightly to the right.

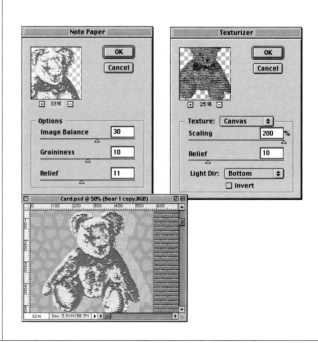

9

Duplicate the 'Bear 2' layer. Make the original 'Bear 2' layer active and choose Image > Adjust > Hue/Saturation to change the hue to the diagram value. Set the layer's blending mode to Color Dodge and Opacity to 50%. Choose the Move tool and shift the image slightly to the right. Make the 'Bear 2 copy' layer active and choose Images > Adjust > Hue/Saturation and set the Hue to -60. Set the layer's blending mode to Hard Light.

10

Select the 'Bear 3' layer. Choose Image > Adjust > Hue/Saturation and set the Hue to the diagram value. Choose Filter > Stylize > Find Edges and repeat the effect.

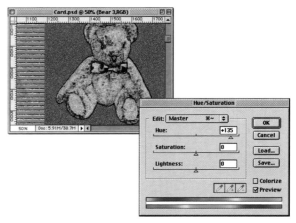

11

Duplicate the 'Bear 4' layer. Make the 'Bear 4 copy' layer active and set the blending mode to Hue and Opacity to 50%. Shift the layer toward the left and down so the bow-tie is offset. Make the original 'Bear 4' layer active, select Images > Adjust > Hue/Saturation and set the options to the diagram values. Reset the foreground and background to the default colors. Choose Filter > Artistic > Palette Knife. Set the blending mode of 'Bear 4' to Luminosity.

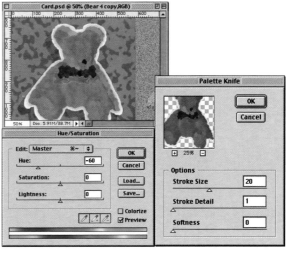

12

Make the 'Bear 5' layer active and choose Filter > Texture > Grain. Set the layer's blending mode to Luminosity.

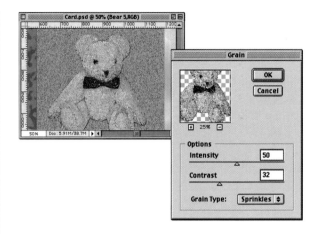

13

Make the 'Bear 6' layer active, choose Images > Adjust > Hue/Saturation and set the Hue to the same settings as in Step 11. Choose Filter > Brush Strokes > Accented Edges and set the options to the diagram values. Choose Filter > Stylize > Glowing Edges and set the options to the diagram values. Duplicate the layer and set Opacity of the 'Bear 6 copy' layer to 20%. Set the blending mode of the original 'Bear 6' layer to Color Dodge and Opacity to 31%.

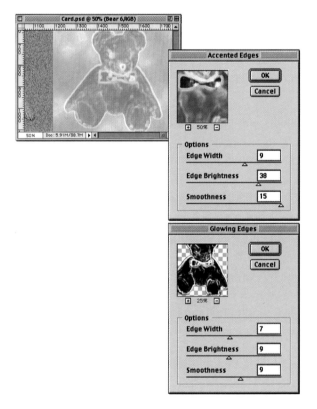

14

Create a new layer immediately above the 'Background' layer named 'Blur.' Hold down the command (Ctrl) key and click on the 'Bear 1 copy' layer in the Layers palette to load its selection. Choose Select > Feather and change the Feather Radius to 8 pixels. Choose a foreground color for blurring. White was chosen for this exercise. Choose Edit > Stroke and set the options to the diagram values. Apply the effect to create a blurred halo around the character, making it appear as if it was floating up off the background. Repeat this process for each bear using complementary colors for the blur layer to complete the image.

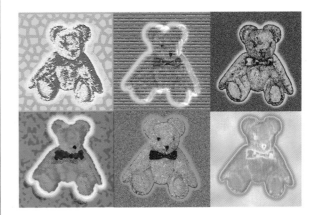

CHANGING BACKGROUNDS AND CHARACTER IMAGES

Try creating a few variations by simplifying the background, choosing different images or changing the special effects.

• Changing the Image

1

Copy just the 'Background' layer of the file created in exercise 2-2 and place it in a new file of the same dimensions and option settings.

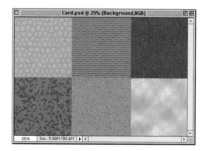

2

Open a file with a different image to use as the pop art icon. For this exercise, open Images > 2-03 > Applications > car.psd on the supplementary CD-ROM. Since the contours of this image are clearly defined, try choosing Filter > Brush Strokes > Accented Edges or use Filter > Stylize > Glowing Edges to exaggerate the outline. We also tried Filter > Artistic > Rough Pastels to obscure the contours and experimented with effects that superimpose layers.

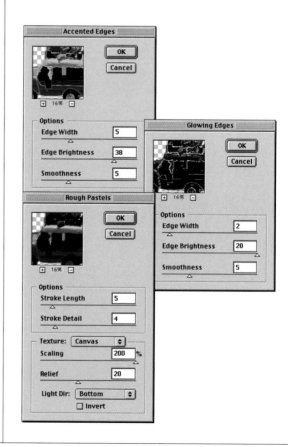

3

Changing the icon and effects creates a substantially different impression, even if the images are aligned similarly. Try different filters to produce your own original effects.

• Leaving the Background White

You can also create interesting compositions by setting the background to white, lining up six copies of the same image as in exercise 2-3 and applying different colors to the copies. Applying a few filters will maintain the atmosphere of the photo, but produce some interesting results.

ARRANGING BACKGROUNDS FORMED BY PHOTOGRAPHS

When creating an illustration that uses a photographic image for the background, it may be wise to select a picture that seems to lack an element. Then apply special effects and add elements to make it more effective.

1

Open the source material images. For this exercise, open Images > 2-04 > duckbill_300.psd or duckbill_150.psd on the supplementary CD-ROM. Since the balloons will be extended beyond the background image in this illustration, blank spaces have already been added above and to the right of the background image in this file. Create a new layer named 'Rainbow.' Choose the Rectangular Marquee tool to select approximately one-third of the photo at the bottom. Choose the Linear Gradient tool and set the options to the diagram values to draw a rainbow at a slight angle and at the width of your choice.

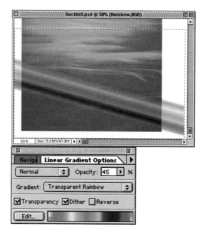

2

Apply another gradient over this one at the same angle, but set Opacity to 20% and make it slightly wider. Hold down the shift (Shift) key and apply another gradient horizontally. Adding numerous gradients together gives the rainbow a softer image compared to the default rainbow gradation alone.

3

Lower the Opacity of the 'Rainbow' layer to about 70%. Hold down the command (Ctrl) key and click on the 'Background Photograph' to load its selection. Reverse the selection (Select > Inverse) and delete the portions of the rainbow extending outside the photo.

4

You will now draw a mountain in the background. First, create a new layer and name it 'Mountains.' Change the foreground color to dark brown (R:98, G:54, B:20). Choose the Polygon Lasso tool to create a selection in the shape of a mountain.

5

Select the Linear Gradient tool and set the options to the diagram values. Drag the tool from the top of the selection down so that the base of the mountains become transparent. You can repeat the same gradient a number of times to give the mountains a denser effect.

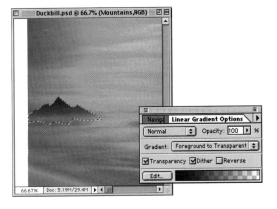

6

You will now construct balls that will become the balloons. First, duplicate the 'Background Photograph' layer. Make the 'Background Photograph copy' layer active and choose Edit > Transform > Numeric. Set both the Width and Height dimensions of the Scale section to 40%. Copy the whole layer.

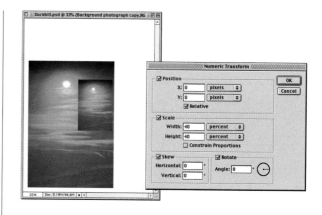

7

Hide the 'Background photograph copy' layer and create a new layer named 'Balloon 1.' Choose the Elliptical Marquee tool and draw a balloon-sized circle where you wish a balloon to be placed. Draw the neck of the balloon as an addition to the circle by choosing the Polygon Lasso tool and holding down the shift (Shift) key while you draw.

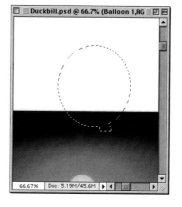

8

Choose Edit > Paste Into to paste the clipboard image into the Step 7 balloon selection. Choose Select > Load Selection to load the mask for this layer and to select the shape of the balloon again.

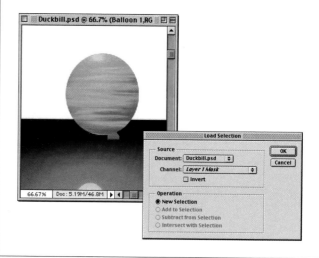

9

Choose Filter > Distort > Spherize and set Amount to 100%. Applying this several times will make the image appear more spherical.

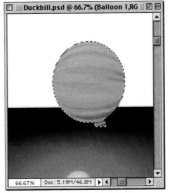
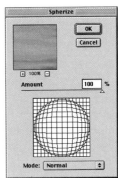

10

Increase the number of balloons by repeating Steps 8 and 9. Change the balloon colors and vary them by coloring some with low opacity settings or by changing the Hue/Saturation settings. If you wish to use the prepared paths for the balloons instead of drawing your own, select each balloon as a sub-path, then change it into a selection before applying Steps 8 and 9. Put darker colored balloons in the background to create a 3-D effect.

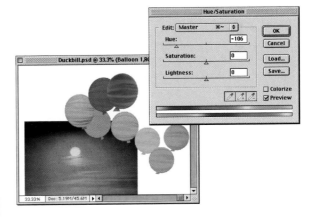

11

Delete the 'Background photograph copy' layer. Create a new layer and change its blending mode to Color Burn. Choose the Airbrush tool and spray areas that need extra gloss. Create another new layer with the blending mode set to Normal. Set the foreground color to white and apply luster with the airbrush. This makes the balloons appear to shine without completely erasing the underlying pattern. Link all the balloon layers together, merge them and name the result 'Balloons.'

12

Next, you will draw the character. In this exercise you will master the technique of filling in pre-saved paths. First, create a new layer named 'Body' above the 'Balloon' layer. Choose the Paths palette and click on 'Duckbill.' Choose the Direct-Selection path tool and select the body outline from the displayed paths. Change the foreground color to earthen yellow (R:235, G:178, B:37) and the background to white. Choose Paths palette menu > Fill Subpath and set the options to the diagram values.

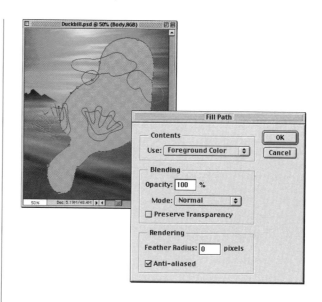

13

Choose Filter > Distort > Glass and set the options to the diagram values. Choose Paths palette menu > Fill Subpath and set Opacity to 50% and fill the subpath again.

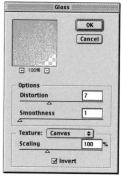

14

Create 'Right Hand' and 'Left Hand' layers. Fill them using the procedures in Steps 12 and 13.

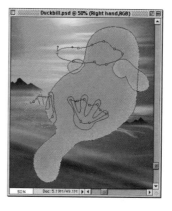

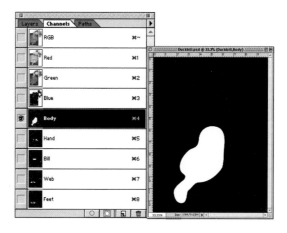

TIPS

If you are drawing a character from scratch, draw the outline using the paths tool and then follow the same procedures to fill it in. Where it is easier to draw freehand lines with tools like the Lasso, first save the selection onto a channel before filling it to achieve the same results.

15

Create a new layer above the hand layers. Select the bill and web paths. Change the foreground color to yellow (R:255, G:191, B:36), choose Fill Subpath as in Step 12, set Opacity to 100% and the blending mode to Normal, and fill the subpaths. Create a 'Feet' layer, select the paths for both feet and fill the subpaths with orange (R: 255, G:150, B:27).

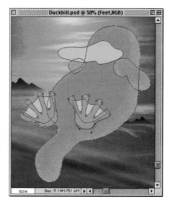

16

You will now add shadows to the hands and feet. Make the 'Body' layer active, choose the Paintbrush tool, select a soft brush and set the options to the diagram values. Choose a color with a slightly lower luminosity than the body (R:172, G:77, B:13), and draw shadows for the hands and feet.

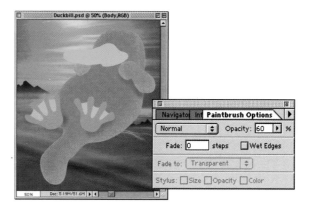

17

Select the 'Bill,' 'Feet' and 'Hand' layers in turn in the Layers palette and load their selections by holding down the command (Ctrl) key and clicking on the respective layers. Use the same paintbrush as in Step 16 to apply shadows. Next, choose Select > Feather and set the Feather Radius to 5 pixels. Set the foreground color to the yellow color used in the web's selection. Choose Edit > Stroke and set the Width to 3 pixels and the Location to Center to blur the surrounding area.

18

Create a new layer above the 'Body' layer. Choose the Elliptical Marquee tool and draw circles on this layer the size of eyes. Reset the foreground and background to their default colors, then switch them. Choose the Radial Gradient tool and set the Gradient to 'Foreground color to Background,' and drag the tool from the top left of the circle to the bottom right. Set the foreground to brown (R:207, G:106, B:18), choose a soft paintbrush and draw the claws on the fingertips. After the character's various parts are just about complete, merge the body and right hand layers, naming the result 'Duckbill 1.' Merge the other remaining layers into one layer named 'Duckbill 2.'

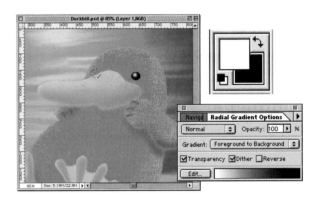

19

Lower the Opacity of the duckbill layers, and create a new layer named 'Balloon Strings 1.' Choose the Pen tool to draw lines for the balloon strings on the right-hand side. Choose a hard-edged 3 pixel brush. Change the foreground color to yellow (R:255, G:255, B:0). Choose Paths palette menu > Stroke Subpath, set the Tool to Paintbrush and click OK. Move the 'Balloon strings 1' layer between the 'Duckbill 1' layer and 'Duckbill 2' layer.

20

Similarly, create a 'Balloon strings 2' layer and draw lines for the left-hand balloon strings. Place this layer beneath the 'Duckbill 1' layer. A path has also been created in the Paths palette for all the strings. To use these paths, select the left strings and right strings separately using the Direct-Selection path tool and perform Steps 19 and 20.

21

Finally, reset the Opacity of the duckbill layers and create an adjustment layer. Make the 'Mountains' layer active as the top layer of the background elements. Choose Layer > New Layer > Adjustment Layer and set Type to Brightness/Contrast. Set the Brightness to -30 to lower the background tones. Merge the separate images to complete the illustration.

FILTERED FANTASIES

Turn photos into fancy artwork easily. This technique is best suited to pictures with large patterns and clearly defined colors.

1

Photos used for this purpose should be scanned at high resolution. For this exercise, you will use an image from the supplementary CD-ROM. Open Images > 2-05 > teatime.psd. Duplicate the 'Background' layer so that you can redo the process in case of error.

©Datacraft

2

Apply filters to the 'Background copy' layer to give it a softer image. First, choose Filter > Blur > Gaussian Blur and set the options to the diagram values to slightly blur the image.

3

Choose Filter > Noise > Median and set the options to the diagram values to blur the color without affecting the shapes. Try different Radius settings to determine the best since the optimal settings will depend on such factors as the elements of the particular photograph and personal taste.

4

You will now transform the colors into pastels with multiple adjustment layers. Since the photo's contrast is low, choose Layer > New Layer > Adjustment Layer to create a new adjustment layer for adjusting the levels. Name the layer 'Level Adjustments.' Choose Image > Adjust > Levels and set the options to the diagram values to increase the contrast.

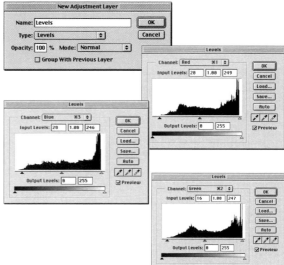

5

Create a new adjustment layer named 'Color Balance' to adjust the color balance in a similar fashion. Set the Midtones to the diagram values to select a fancy coloration with lots of red and yellow.

6

To accentuate the pastel impression, create a new adjustment layer to adjust the levels and apply the settings shown in the diagram. Name the layer 'Level Adjustments 2.'

7

Add in some color splotches to bring out the feel of an illustration since the overall coloring is somewhat muted. Keep the 'Level Adjustments 2' layer active and set the foreground color to black. Choose the Airbrush tool and try brushes of varying sizes set to Opacity of 40% to add color here and there.

8

Create a new adjustment layer with the Type set to Hue/Saturation. Increase the Saturation using the settings in the diagram to freshen the colors.

9

Now add the finishing touches with outline strokes and colors. Create a new layer named 'Coloring.' Create a new brush with a Diameter of 17 pixels, a Hardness of 0%, a Spacing of 25%, an Angle of 0% and a Roundness of 100%. Choose the Airbrush tool and select the new brush to draw beige and brown outlines and white and cream highlights to complete the image.

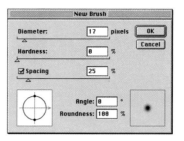

TURNING PHOTOS INTO PAINTINGS - THE FIND EDGES TECHNIQUE

This method of transforming photographs into illustrations is the best for those who find design and sketching difficult. Apply filters to a photograph to give the impression of a coloring book image.

1

Photos used for this purpose should be scanned at high resolution. For this exercise, you will use an image from the supplementary CD-ROM. Open Images > 2-06 > fruits.psd. Open the Channels palette and compare the red, green and blue channels to select the brightest channel with the clearest outlines. Red is the color to select for this exercise.

©Datacraft

2

Duplicate the selected channel to create a new alpha channel 1. Name the new channel 'Outline preparation.'

160

3

Keep the 'Outline' channel active and choose Filter > Stylize > Find Edges. The outline will be drawn as a grayscale image.

4

Change the foreground color to white, choose the Airbrush tool and select narrow brushes to erase areas other than the main outlines that are not required in the channel.

5

Display the Layers palette. Choose Select > Load Selection, place a check in the Invert check box and load the 'Outline' channel. Make the 'Background' layer active and copy and paste the selection. Name the new layer 'Outline.'

6

Choose Filter > Other > Minimum and set the Radius to 1 pixel to thicken the outline. Set layer's blending mode to Multiply.

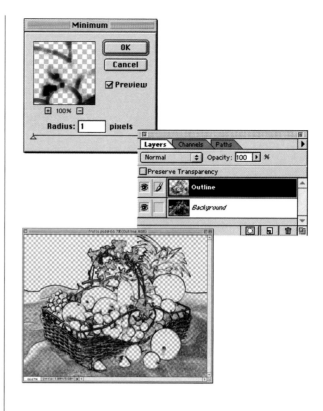

7

Create a new layer beneath the outline layer named 'Coloring 1.' Fill the entire layer with white. Decrease Opacity to view the photograph underneath, choose the Airbrush tool and select one of the larger brushes with the options set to the diagram values. Color the illustration with your choice of foreground colors, lightening and darkening them where appropriate.

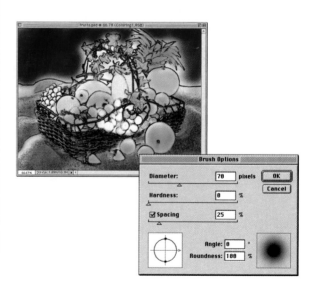

8

Create a new layer called 'Coloring 2' above the 'Coloring 1' layer so that you can return to the previous step in case the coloring is unsuccessful. Choose a brush of 20 pixels to color the smaller areas. Add highlights to give the illustration a 3-D effect.

9

Finally, create a new layer named 'Coloring 3.' Select a brush of 10 to 15 pixels to draw detailed shadows and highlights on the leaves. Set the foreground color to white and add highlights using a thin airbrush of about 10 pixels. Use extremely thin brushes to add seeds to the strawberries and net patterns to the melons to add more life.

CHANGING IMAGES WITH FILTERS

Applying filters to an image will produce a different atmosphere. Photoshop's default filters are used in this exercise. Try numerous variations by changing the settings and using different filters.

Pastel Drawing

Merge the layers, then choose Filter > Artistic > Rough Pastels and set the options to the diagram values.

Stippling

Merge the layers, then set the foreground color to light orange (R:246, G:126, B:66) and choose Filter > Pixelate > Pointillize and set the options to the diagram values.

Granulation

Merge the layers, then choose Filter > Texture > Grain and set the options to the diagram values.

Crosshatching

Merge the layers, then choose Filter > Brush Strokes > Crosshatch and set the options to the diagram values.

CHRISTMAS CARDS

There are many ways to use an illustration if the layers are left unmerged in a file. The characters can be used in combination with logos or the background can be printed by itself. You can even create a pop-up card with relative ease like the one shown here.

T-SHIRTS

It is easy to make an original T-shirt design by printing on to heat transfer papers that can be applied to the shirt with an iron. Don't forget to reverse the contents left to right to a mirror image if you wish to include text.

Equipment supplied by Alps Electric Co., Ltd. (Photo Color Printer MD-1300J/D)

Chapter ②

CALENDARS

Rather than just printing out your work, why not put it to practical use in a calendar? Personalize it by marking holidays and special anniversaries.

FREEHAND

People won't believe you when you tell them you used Photoshop to create these pictures. With its incredible array of brushes and countless filters, you can create amazing effects when you use Photoshop not only on your photos, but on your freehand drawings too.

Transform mediocre drawings into artwork with a completely different flavor simply by processing them in various ways with Photoshop. If you lack the confidence to draw, you can practice with a coloring-book style on the prepared paths available on the supplementary CD-ROM.

PATCHWORK-STYLE ILLUSTRATIONS USING TEXTURES

Try giving interesting textures to patchwork compositions. This exercise also introduces the technique of producing 3-D effects with adjustment layers.

1

Create a new file that is 6.5 x 8 cm (approximately 770 x 950 pixels). Set the Resolution to 300 ppi and the Contents to Transparent. Create a new layer named 'Sketch,' choose the Paintbrush tool and draw a rough sketch that will become your line drawing. We have used the line drawing available on the supplementary CD-ROM by opening Images > 3-01 folder > patch.psd. Set the blending mode of the 'Sketch' layer to Multiply and Opacity to approximately 20%.

TIPS

It is difficult to achieve natural-looking sketches when drawing with a computer mouse. If you have access to a scanner or digital camera, sketch on paper first and scan the results. You can also create your own texture files by scanning various items to augment the pre-created textures provided for these exercises.

2

Create a new layer beneath the 'Sketch' layer named 'Background.' Set the foreground color to cream (R:255, G:255, B:204) and the background to green (R:132, G:254, B:100). Choose the Linear Gradient tool, set the Gradient option to 'Foreground color to Background' and drag from the top left corner to the bottom right corner.

3

Copy the 'Background' layer. Set the foreground color to pink (R:255, G:153, B:153). Choose the Airbrush tool and define a brush with a Diameter of 100 pixels and a Hardness of 0%. Click anywhere in the image to make a pattern. Next, set the foreground color to yellow (R:255, G:204, B:0). Define a brush with a Diameter of 200 pixels and a Hardness of 0%. Apply the brush anywhere in the image to add to the pattern.

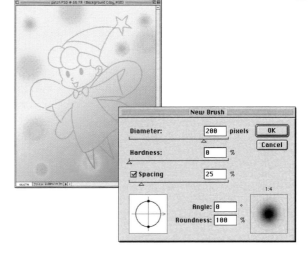

4

Now add patterns to the character. First, open a suitable texture file for the wings, select all and copy. In this exercise, we used Images > 3-01 > Materials > pattern3.psd on the supplementary CD-ROM. Reselect the file containing the character. Paste the selection and name the resulting new layer 'Wings.' Move the new layer beneath the 'Sketch' layer. If the texture selection is too small to cover the wings, enlarge it using Edit > Transform > Scale.

5

Select the outline of the wings using the Lasso tool or trace its path and convert the path to a selection over the top of the sketch lines. Keep the 'Wings' layer active and choose Layer > Add Layer Mask > Reveal Selection. Both the image icon and mask icon will appear on the 'Wings' layer of the Layers palette. Click the link button between the two to delete it.

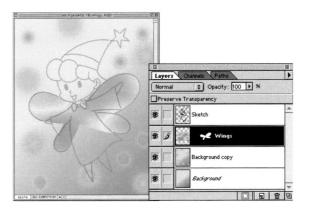

171

6

Create 'Hat,' 'Hat Ornament,' 'Hair,' 'Clothes' and 'Star and Ribbon' layers with the same procedures. Create a 'Face, Hands and Legs' layer immediately above the 'Wings' layer. Fill this layer with a skin color (R:255, G:220, B:177) without adding a texture.

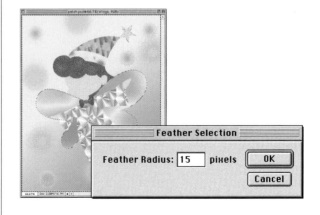

7

When the patterns of all the parts are complete, drag the mask icon off each layer onto the Trash Can icon, located at the bottom of the Layers palette. A dialog box will appear asking whether or not to apply the mask. Click the Apply button to cut the texture in the shape of the mask.

8

Now add shadows to each part. First, hold down the command (Ctrl) key and click on the 'Wings' layer in the Layers palette to load its selection. Choose Select > Inverse to reverse the selection. Choose Select > Feather and set the Feather Radius to 15 pixels to blur the inverse selection.

9

Create a new adjustment layer by choosing Layer > New layer > Adjustment Layer. Set the Type to Levels and place a check in the Group With Previous Layer check box. Set the Input Levels to the diagram values to apply shadows to the edges. Since the required adjustment levels will vary among patterns, adjust them according to your preferences.

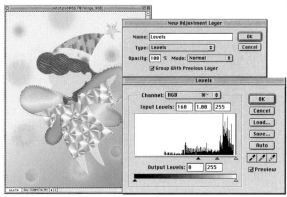

10

Create an adjustment layer for each layer, and create a new layer after the shadows are applied. Choose a Paintbrush tool and draw in the face using the sketch for guidance. Finally, delete the 'Sketch' layer to complete the image.

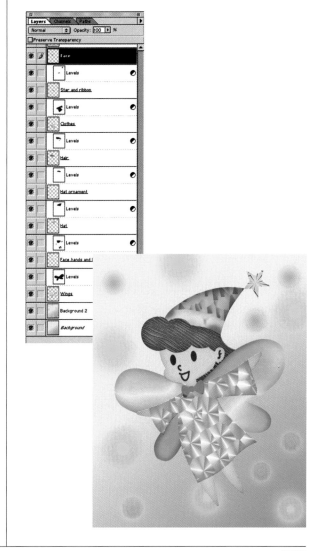

BUILDING WITH LAYERS

Make a number of separate face parts, like eyes and noses, on different layers, to create interchangeable faces. You can even generate new ideas for characters by making numerous parts and trying out the various combinations.

1

Create a new file that is 500 x 600 pixels. Set the Resolution to 300 ppi and the Contents to White. Start by drawing the outline. Create a new layer named 'Face.' Choose the Elliptical Marquee tool and draw a circle. Switch to the Rectangular Marquee tool, hold down the option (Alt) key to select the right half of the circle and delete it.

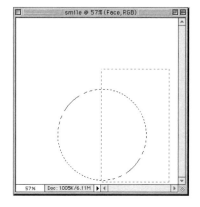

2

Hold down the shift (Shift) key and add to the selection using the Rectangular Marquee tool to draw a rectangle the same width as the radius of the semicircle. Fill the selection with a skin color (R:255, G:199, B:146). Copy and paste it. Choose Edit > Transform > Flip Horizontal, and position the left and right selections together. Choose Layer > Merge Down to combine the layers.

3

Load the 'Face' layer selection. Choose the Airbrush tool and add a shadow along the outline with a darker skin color (R: 253, G:166, B:103). Deselect the selection. Place a check in the Preserve Transparency check box. Set the foreground color to pink (R:255, G:112, B:122), choose the Airbrush tool and paint blush on the cheeks. Add highlights to the cheeks with white.

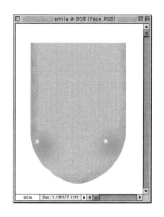

TIPS

The area deleted from the circle in Step 1 will determine whether the face is round, triangular or another shape. For practice, try creating different faces, such as those with thin or full outlines or those that have a feminine or masculine appearance.

4

Create a new layer named 'Eye.' Choose the Elliptical Marquee tool, draw a circle and fill it with white. Set the foreground color to light pink (R:226, G:172, B:172). Choose the Radial Gradient tool, set the options to the diagram values and apply the gradient from the center of the eye outward.

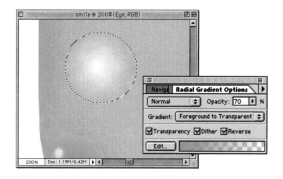

5

Draw a circular selection that will become the pupil. Set the foreground color to dark brown (R:90, G:2, B:0) and the background color to light brown (R:154, G:58, B:22). Choose the Linear Gradient tool, set the options to the diagram values and apply the gradient from the top left to the bottom right.

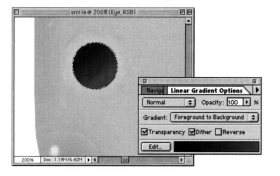

6

Deselect the selection. Set the foreground color to black. Choose the Paintbrush tool, select one of the larger brushes and click on the center of the eye to draw a circle. Change to a smaller brush and draw two white dots, one larger than the other, on the pupil.

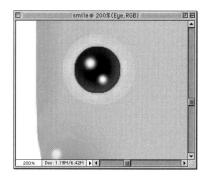

7

After one eye is complete, duplicate the 'Eye' layer. Hold down the command + shift (Ctrl + Shift) keys and move the selection over to where the right eye should be. Rename the 'Eye' layer 'Right Eye' and the 'Eye Copy' layer 'Left eye.' If you wish to place both eyes on one layer, make the 'Eye' layer active, link the 'Eye Copy' layer to it and merge the layers.

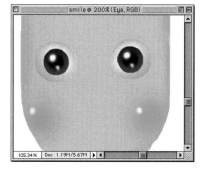

TIPS

A simple method of duplicating the right eye on the same layer as the left, is to select the left eye, hold down the shift + option (Shift + Alt) keys and drag the selection.

8

Next, create a new layer named 'Eyebrow.' Set the foreground color to brown (R:69, G:2, B:1). Choose the Paintbrush tool and select one of the thinner brushes to draw an eyebrow. After one eyebrow is complete, choose Layer > Duplicate Layer. Choose Edit > Transform > Flip Horizontal, then determine the placement of the eyebrow. As with the 'Eye' layer, you may either combine the two eyebrows in one layer or give each a name and save them in separate layers.

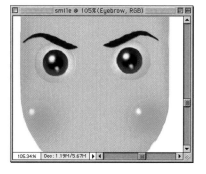

9

Create a new layer named 'Nose.' Choose the Lasso tool and draw the nose shape. Hold down the option (Alt) key if you wish to draw a straight line. Choose the Eyedropper tool and set the foreground color to the same skin color as the face. Fill in the nose and set the foreground color to pink (R:255, G:112, B:122). Set the Linear Gradient tool to the same settings as in Step 5 and apply it lightly to the tip of the nose.

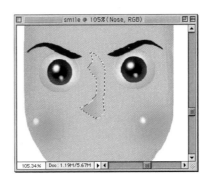

10

Create a new layer named 'Mouth.' Choose the Elliptical Marquee tool and draw a vertical ellipse. Switch to the Rectangular Marquee tool, hold down the option (Alt) key and select the top half of the ellipse, then delete that area. Fill the selection with red (R:153, G:0, B:0).

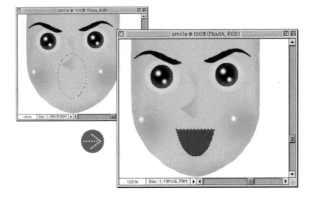

11

Deselect the selection and place a check in the Preserve Transparency check box on the Layers palette. Choose the Elliptical Marquee tool and select a semicircle covering the lower part of the mouth. Hold down the option (Alt) key while you draw a small ellipse and cut out part of the selection to be the throat. Select the remaining tongue area and color it pink (R:255, G:0, B:52).

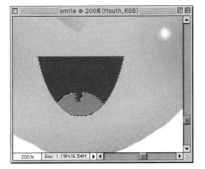

12

Create a new layer above the 'Mouth' layer. Choose the Rectangular Marquee tool and draw a small square selection. Fill it with white. Set the foreground color to dark pink (R:195, G:115, B:115). Choose the Linear Gradient tool, set the options to the diagram values and drag from the top right toward the bottom left.

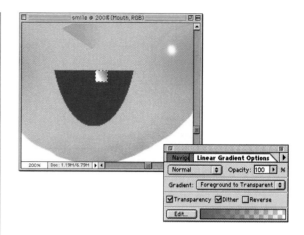

13

Keep the tooth created in Step 12 selected, hold down the option (Alt) key, choose the Move tool and drag the tooth to duplicate it on the same layer. Repeat and line up the teeth. Choose the Blur tool, set the Pressure to about 70% and blur the area between the teeth as well as their outlines. Adjust the overall composition of the teeth with such commands as Edit > Transform > Distort. Merge the layer with the 'Mouth' layer below it.

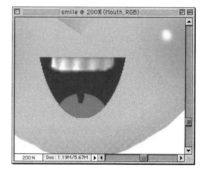

14

Create a new layer named 'Ears' and move it beneath the 'Face' layer. Choose the Eyedropper tool and select the same skin color as the face. Choose the Paintbrush tool and draw a rough outline of an ear. Choose the Magic Wand tool and select the ear. Set the foreground color to orange (R:255, G:117, B:21) and add shadows with the Airbrush tool.

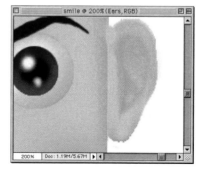

15

When one ear is complete, choose the Move tool, hold down the option + shift (Alt + Shift) keys and move the ear to where the other ear should be placed. This will duplicate it on the same layer. Choose Edit > Transform > Flip Horizontal to make them symmetrical. Choose the Move tool and adjust the placement of the ears.

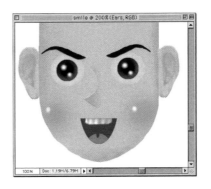

16

Next, draw the neck. Create a new layer named 'Neck' and move it beneath the 'Face' layer. Choose the Rectangular Marquee tool and draw a selection that will become the neck. As with the ears, fill the area with skin color before applying shadows with the Airbrush tool.

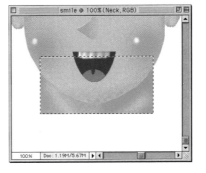

17

Lastly, create a new layer named 'Hair' and move it to the very top of the Layers palette. Choose the Polygon Lasso tool and draw half of the hair. Fill it with yellow (R:253, G:200, B:0).

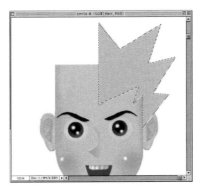

18

When half the hair is complete, choose the Move tool, hold down the option + shift (Alt + Shift) keys and move it to where the other half should be placed to duplicate it on the same layer. Choose Edit > Transform > Flip Horizontal so that the two halves are placed symmetrically. Use the Move tool and adjust the hair placement. If the hair does not match the size of the head, choose Edit > Transform > Scale to adjust the size.

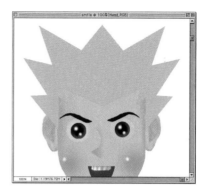

19

To apply shadows to the hair, choose the Polygon Lasso tool, hold down the shift (Shift) key and choose all of the areas to be shadowed at once. Paint the selected areas with orange (R:230, G:135, B:0). Choose the Blur tool, set the Pressure to 70% and blur the borders between the yellow and orange areas. If you wish to add shadows with the Airbrush tool, apply the shadows after placing a check in the Preserve Transparency check box in the Layers palette.

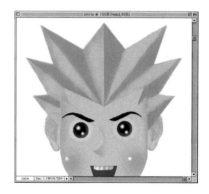

20

Reduce the Opacity of the 'Hair' layer to show the 'Ears' layer. If there are any overlapping areas, use the Eraser tool to erase them. All that remains is to clean up the border between the hair and head and the face is complete.

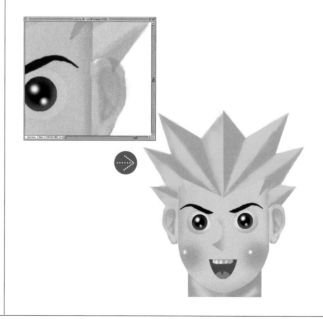

21

Create new faces with the same procedures based on the layers of your illustration. Try shifting the position of the face parts, hiding layers and drawing new replacement parts, then copy and paste different face parts into different files to create a lineup of original characters. For reference, open Images > 3-02 > faces_300.psd or faces_150.psd on the supplementary CD-ROM to see pre-created examples.

SYMBOLIC BACKGROUNDS

Symbol fonts are often available as freeware. Experiment with incorporating them into your designs

1

Start by creating a background. Create a new file that is 1,800 x 1,800 pixels. Set the Resolution to 300 ppi and the Contents to Transparent. If your computer system has limited memory, set the resolution lower to make the file size smaller. Rename 'Layer 1' to 'Background' and fill it with a color of your choice. In this example we have used cream (R:255, G:255, B:208). Choose the Airbrush tool and draw a pattern for the background with your choice of colors. Change the color and add to the pattern.

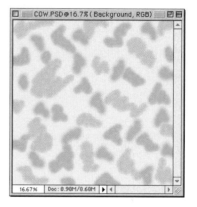

2

Choose Filter > Distort > Ocean Ripple, set the options to the diagram options and apply it to the entire background. The diagram shows the settings for a 300 dpi image; adjust your settings to suit the resolution you have selected.

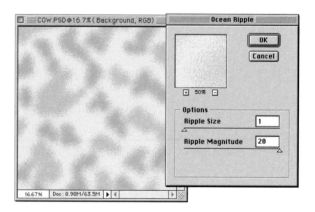

3

Next, draw the character. Create a new layer named 'Sketch.' Hide the 'Background' layer. Select an easily distinguished color for the foreground color. Choose the Pencil tool and draw a rough sketch.

4

Create a new layer beneath the 'Under Sketch' layer. Fill in each part separately and save it on a separate layer, giving it a corresponding name, such as 'Head,' 'Ears' or 'Body.' Choose the Elliptical Marquee tool and join several curved selections together (shift (Shift) key) to select the curved portions of the under-sketch. If you are accustomed to the Path tool, transform the selection to a path to compose the shapes. To make certain body parts symmetrical, such as the ears and eyes, draw one on a new layer, copy and paste it, then select Edit > Transform > Flip Horizontal before placing it in the position of your choice. Hide the 'Under Sketch' layer.

5

Choose Filter > Blur > Gaussian and set the Radius to 3 pixels. Place a check in the Preserve Transparency check box on the Layers palette. Choose the Airbrush tool, select one of the larger brushes and apply shadows and patterns. Determine from which side the light should shine and trace the outline of each part, slightly darkening the color to create highlights and shadows.

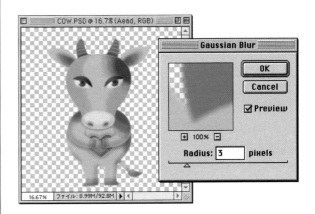

6

Create a new layer named 'Glasses' above the 'Head' layer. Choose the Elliptical Marquee tool and draw two oval selections that will become the lens frames. Choose the Paths palette and click the 'Make work path from selection' icon to create a path. Choose the Freeform Pen tool and draw the remainder of the glasses frame and save it as the 'Glasses' path.

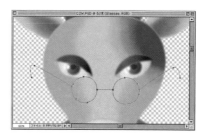

Freeform Pen

7

Set the foreground color to navy blue (R:0, G:132, B:171). Choose the Paintbrush tool and select the brush in the diagram. Choose Paths palette menu > Stroke Path and set the Tools option to Paintbrush. Choose Paths palette menu > Turn Off Path.

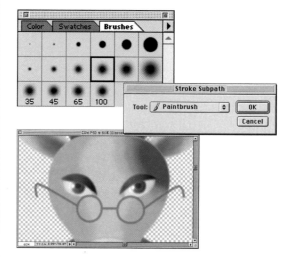

8

Add some depth to the eyes. Set the fore-ground color to white and add highlights in the direction from which the light is coming. Choose the Elliptical Marquee tool and select the eye. Choose Filter > Render > Lighting Effects and set the options to the diagram values to add expression to the eyes. This will complete the character. Link all the bull's parts, merge the layers by choosing Layers palette menu > Merge Visible and rename the result 'Bull.'

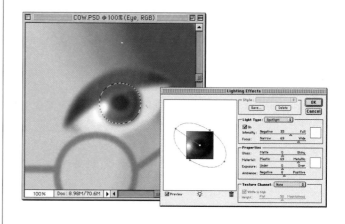

9

Create a new layer. Set the background to your choice of color for the scattered symbols and name the layer something like 'Green Symbols.' Choose the Text tool and input the symbols into the text box, placing a space between each. Choose Layer > Type > Rasterize. Choose the Lasso tool and select each symbol separately, then place it in the position of your choice. For this example we have used a font called 'CropBats.' A compressed file containing this font can be found in the supplementary CD-ROM.

10

To apply blurs in varying directions, place the symbols onto three separate layers of different colors. Further duplicate each layer so that one of each pair can be used for blurring, creating a total of six symbol layers.

11

Make the lower layer of the duplicated symbol layers active, choose Filter > Blur > Motion Blur and set the options to the diagram values to add moving shadows. Make the symbols appear to be in motion by changing the Angle and Distance for each layer. In this example, we used 45° and 410 pixels, -55° and 310 pixels, and -28° and 410 pixels for the respective layers. Move the symbols to the places most appropriate for the entire image, then merge the six symbol layers into one.

TIPS

Interesting background designs can be created by scattering royalty-free postscript images in the background even if special symbol fonts are unavailable to you.

CropBats AOE Font designed by Brian J. Bonislawsky, Astigmatic One Eye Foundry, © 1997-1998.

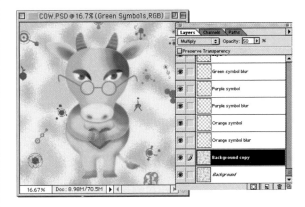

12

To add depth to the layered textures in the background, duplicate the entire 'Background' layer, change the blending mode of the 'Background copy' layer to Multiply and set the Opacity to 50%. Choose Filter > Distort > Glass and set the options to the diagram values.

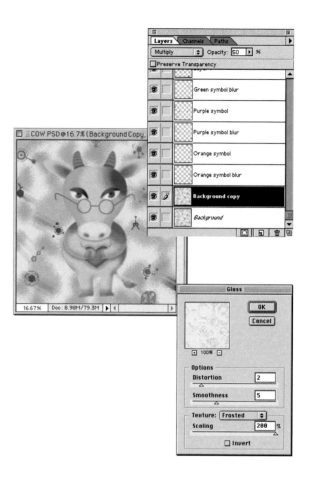

13

Choose Filter > Distort > Displace, and set the options in the Displace dialog to the diagram values. Then choose a displacement map by opening the Photoshop 5.0 folder and choosing Plug-ins > Displacement Maps > Free Lines (25%). Choose Edit > Transform > Rotate 90° CW to rotate the layer. Since the lower texture can also be seen, the overlapping textures will have a pastel appearance. The image is now complete.

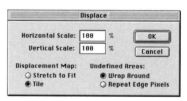

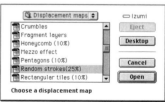

CHANGING THE COLOR OF A CHARACTER

Adding layers to change colors.

1

Make the 'Bull' layer active and duplicate it. Choose Filter > Noise > Add Noise. Choose Filter > Artistic > Poster Edges and set the options to the diagram values.

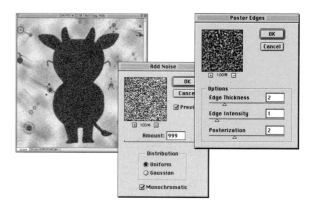

2

Reduce the Opacity to about 60%. Choose the Eraser tool, set the tool in the Eraser Options palette to Airbrush and select a large brush to erase the detailed areas and areas where you want a 3-D look. Choose Image > Adjust > Variations and change the image to a brown color as shown in the diagram.

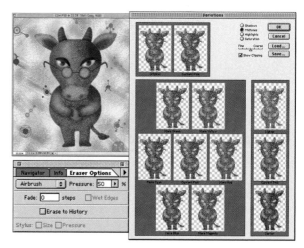

3

Make the original 'Bull' layer active. Choose the Magic Wand tool and click the heart several times on different hues to select the entire object. Copy and paste the selection to create a 'Heart' layer. Hide the 'Bull' layer. Choose the Eraser tool, set the tool in the Eraser Options palette to Pencil and select a fine brush to draw cracks in the heart.

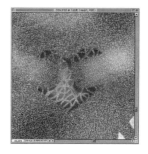

4

Copy the 'Bull' layer again. Choose Image > Adjust > Hue/Saturation for the original layer and reduce the Saturation to -100 to produce a monochrome image.

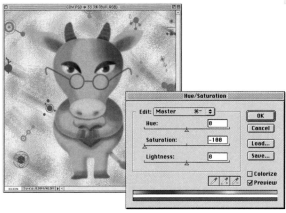

5

You will use the 'Bull copy 2' to show break-through color in sections of the monochrome image. Choose Hue/Saturation, set the Hue to -173 and both the Saturation and Brightness to 0 to create a light brown bull. Set the Opacity to 70%.

6

Make all the layers visible. Keep the 'Bull copy 2' layer active and choose Layer > Add Layer Mask > Hide All to mask it. Choose the Paintbrush tool and erase only the masked portions within the character that you wish to accent with color, such as the horns and below the eyes. When your central character stands out sufficiently, you are finished.

ADDING HAND-DRAWN TOUCHES

Try creating characters that feature a hand-drawn, slightly blurred appearance created solely with filters.

1

 Create a new file that is 10 x 13 cm (approximately 1,200 x 1,500 pixels). Set the Resolution to 300 ppi and the Contents to Transparent. Use a lower resolution if your computer system has limited memory. Start by drawing a frame that will become the background. Rename 'Layer 1' as 'Frame.' Choose the Rectangular Marquee tool and select a rectangle big enough to be the outer rim of the frame. Hold down the option (Alt) key and select the inner rim of the frame. Set the foreground to the color you wish for the frame. Fill the selection. In this example, we chose yellow (R:246, G:200, B:78).

2

Double-click on the foreground color icon to open the Color Picker dialog box. Slightly shift the Color Picker cursor left and down to drop the brightness and saturation. In this example, we changed the color settings to (R:164, G:130, B:44). Choose the Polygon Lasso tool and create a selection like the one shown in the diagram for each area.

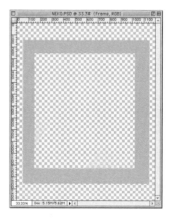

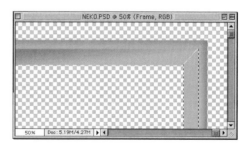

3

Choose the Linear Gradient tool, set the options to the diagram values and drag from left to right in the first selection. Change the direction and stroke length for the gradient in each area to create the best 3-D appearance. In this example, we changed the foreground color twice and created three contours for the frame.

TIPS

Using guides to insert support lines makes selecting easier.

4

Next, create the mirror inside the frame. Create a new layer named 'Mirror' and place it beneath the 'Frame' layer. Choose the Rectangular Marquee tool and select a rectangle slightly bigger than the mirror area. Fill it with light blue (R:169, G:212, B:239). Select the areas shown in the diagram, set the foreground color to white, and apply gradients to different areas as in the previous steps to create the impression of light reflecting off the mirror.

TIPS

The light reflection effect can be strengthened by reducing the Opacity settings and applying the gradient several times. In this example, we applied the gradient once from the bottom left and twice from the top right.

5

Now draw leaves around the frame on a new 'Leaves' layer. Set the foreground color to green (R:44, G:172, B:65). Choose the Paintbrush tool, set the Opacity to 100% and select a hard-edged brush. Alternatively, you can choose the Lasso tool and draw the leaf outlines and fill them.

6

Reduce the brightness and hue of the foreground color. Choose the Lasso tool and select areas for darkening as shown in the diagram. Apply gradations from the center of the leaf outward.

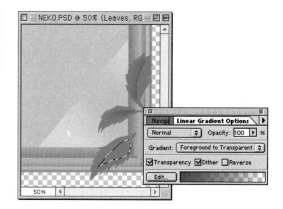

7

Choose a Paintbrush tool with a slightly reduced Opacity to draw the stems. Choose the Elliptical Marquee tool and draw circles at the end of the stems, set the foreground color to the color of the berries and fill the selections. In this example, we used green (R:19, G:118, B:65) and blue (R:73, G:61, B:113). Place a check in the Preserve Transparency check box, slightly reduce the brightness of the foreground color, choose the Airbrush tool and add shadows. Next, increase the brightness of the foreground color and apply luster to the top left of each item.

8

Choose Filter > Artistic > Plastic Wrap and set the options to the diagram values. Emphasizing 3-D aspects at this stage will make the 'hand-drawn' effects more convincing.

9

Make the 'Frame' layer active. Choose Filter > Texture > Craquelure, set the options to the diagram values and apply a bumpy texture to the frame to make it appear more realistic.

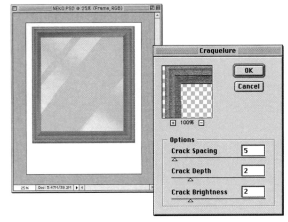

10

Create a new layer named 'Cat.' Choose the Paintbrush tool, set the Opacity to 100% and draw a selection for the cat. Fill it in completely, leaving no patchy areas. Alternatively, choose either the Pen or Lasso tool, draw the outline, fill it and use the Paintbrush tool with a soft-edged brush to blur the outline, giving it a furry look.

11

Create a new layer above the 'Cat' layer. Draw the ears, eyes, and other features with either the Lasso or Paintbrush tool, and fill them. Change the brightness and saturation of the foreground color, then apply shadows with the Paintbrush tool. Draw the whiskers and mouth with a soft-edged brush. When the drawing is complete, merge the layer with the 'Cat' layer.

12

You will now record 'hand-drawn' effects to the Actions palette and apply the action separately to each part of the illustration. First, make the 'Leaves' layer active and choose Actions palette menu > New Action. Name it 'Hand Drawn' and click the Record button. Choose Filter > Noise > Add Noise and set the Amount to 44, the Distribution to Uniform and place a check in the Grayscale check box.

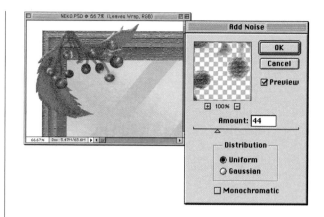

13

Choose Filter > Artistic > Sponge and set the options to the diagram values.

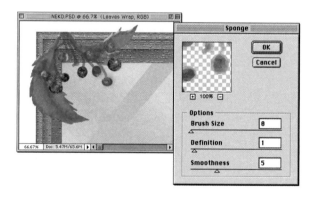

14

Choose Filter > Artistic > Rough Sketch and set the options to the diagram values. Click the Stop button on the Actions palette. Make each of the other layers active in turn and play the action to give them a softer, hand-drawn look.

TIPS

The action file is included on the supplementary CD-ROM. Open Images > 3-04 > 'cat.atn.' You can apply this effect easily by loading this action file. See p37 for instructions on using action files.

REFLECTIONS AND SHADOWS

To apply shadows to the face, leaves and the character, duplicate each layer, shift it slightly and decrease the Opacity of the copy.

1

Start with the frame. Create a copy layer and place it beneath the original. Shift the layer slightly, set its blending mode to Color Burn and Opacity to 30%. Create two layers for the leaves; one for those reflecting in the mirror and one for those casting shadows onto the frame. For the shadows on the frame, set the blending mode to Color Burn and Opacity to 50%. For the mirror reflection, set Opacity to 30%.

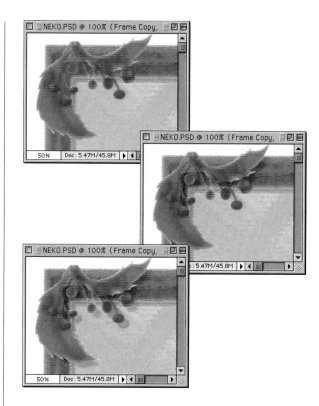

2

Choose the Eraser tool and erase any areas that detract from the appearance of the shadows. Create two duplicate layers for the cat's shadow too. Set the Opacity of the respective layers to 30% and 10% and offset them slightly from the original cat image. The tail will appear more natural if it is cut from the two new layers and offset independently.

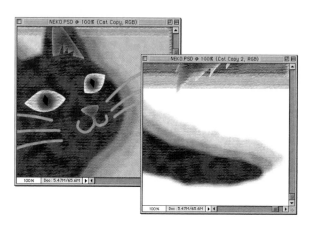

3

Finally, duplicate the 'Mirror' layer and place it above the original layer. Choose Filter > Pixelate > Crystallize and set the options to the diagram values to add a faint texture to the glass. Although the Opacity of the layer is reduced to 13% so that the texture of any one portion of the glass is barely discernible, the glass covers such a large area that the effect changes the feeling of the image. Apply the hand-drawn effect to the rest of the image to complete the illustration.

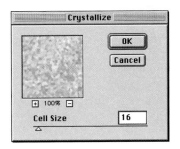

IMPROVISING WITH
REPEATED DESIGNS

Experiment by drawing one scene and using it in a variety of different ways. Practice drawing characters piece by piece.

1

Create a new file that is approximately 1,200 x 700 pixels (10 x 6 cm). Set the Resolution to 300 ppi and Contents to Transparent. Use a lower resolution if your computer system has limited memory. Select the Linear Gradient tool and click the Edit button of the Gradient Tool Options palette to display the Gradient Editor. Choose New and name the result something like 'South Pole.' Set the options to the diagram values to apply a three-color gradient. From the left, set the colors to blue (R:0, G:144, B:176), blue-green (R:0, G:142, B:157) and navy blue (R:0, G:45, B:106). Drag the cursor from the very top to about the middle to apply the gradient.

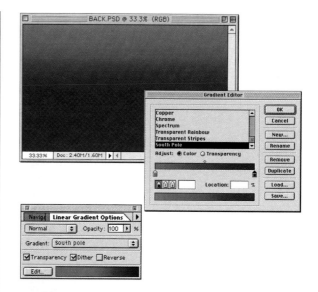

2

Create a new layer named 'Scenery.'Choose the Polygon Lasso tool and draw iceberg outlines. Draw the icebergs in order from the farthest to the closest. Choose the Linear Gradient tool and set the foreground colors to tones such as sky blue (R:24, G:140, B:192) and light blue (R:141, G:209, B:234). Set the Gradient option to 'Foreground to Transparent' and drag from the top to the bottom.

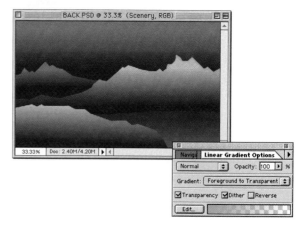

TIPS

To add selections, hold down the shift (Shift) key while making successive selections. To delete sections of a selection, hold down the option (Alt) key and select.

3

Set the foreground color to white. Choose the Polygon Lasso tool and select several areas in the closest iceberg. Choose the Linear Gradient tool, set the Gradient option to 'Foreground color to Transparent' and drag within the selections to create highlights in the iceberg. Set the foreground color to ocean blue (R:63, G:145, B:182), and create shadows at the peaks of the icebergs the same way.

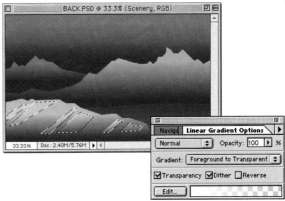

4

Now draw the reflection of the iceberg on the water. Choose the Rectangular Marquee tool and select the area of the iceberg that will reflect on the water. Copy and paste the selection, naming the new layer 'Reflection.' Choose Edit > Transform > Flip Vertical.

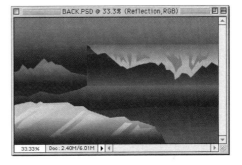

5

Choose the Move tool and position the reflection. After you have positioned it, reduce Opacity to 20% to increase the realism of the reflection. Use the Eraser tool and erase any unneeded portions, particularly where the reflection overlaps other icebergs.

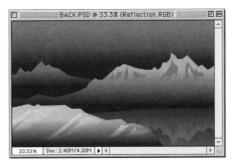

6

Create a new layer named 'Moon and stars.' Set the foreground color to white. Choose the Elliptical Marquee or Paintbrush tool and draw a number of stars. To draw the moon, first choose the Elliptical Marquee tool and draw an ellipse, then hold down the option (Alt) key and select a second ellipse that overlaps the first. The result will be resemble the shape of a crescent moon. Next, fill in the moon. Reduce the Opacity of the 'Moon and Stars' layer to 50% and choose Layer > Merge Visible. Save the file as 'Scenery.' You can find a copy of the 'Scenery' file on the supplementary CD-ROM by opening Images > 3-05 > back_300.psd or back_150.psd.

7

Select and copy all of 'Scenery.' Create a new file that is approximately 1,200 x 1,600 pixels (10 x 13 cm) and set the Contents to White. Paste the 'Scenery' image copied earlier and move it toward the bottom of the canvas. Choose Select > All and choose Filter > Distort > Spherize. Adjust the Amount and apply the filter. A moderately curved surface resembling a cup is appropriate. In this example, we set the Amount option to 42%.

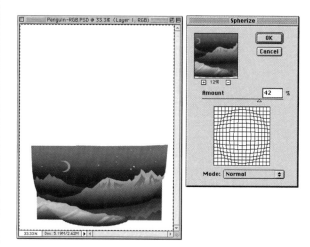

8

When you achieve the shape of an ideal cup, choose the Lasso tool and select and delete areas not required for the cup. Rename the layer 'Cup.'

9

Create a new layer beneath the 'Cup' layer, and set the foreground color to cream (R:255, G:242, B:210). Choose the Elliptical Marquee or Lasso tool and create the handle, the top and bottom rims, the inside edges and the cup interior. Put them on separate layers with names such as 'Handle,' 'Rims,' 'Thickness' and 'Inside,' respectively. Paint the surface of the liquid brown (R:115, G:76, B:17) to resemble coffee.

10

Make the 'Rims' layer active and load its selection by holding down the command (Ctrl) key and clicking on it in the Layers palette. Set the foreground color to a slightly darker cream (R:222, G:194, B:154). Choose the Linear Gradient tool, set the Gradient to 'Foreground to Transparent,' and add a shadow by dragging the tool from the right-hand side.

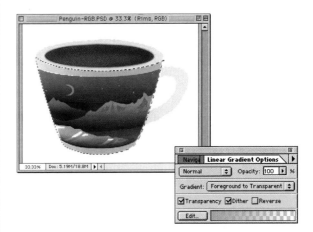

11

Hold down the command (Ctrl) key and click on the 'Inside' layer to load its selection. Choose the Magic Wand tool, hold down the option (Alt) key and select only the inner rim of the cup by clicking on the coffee portion. As in Step 10, add a shadow with the gradient starting from the right, as shown in the diagram.

12

Choose the 'Rim' layer as in Step 11, and this time add a shadow by applying the gradient from the left-hand side.

13

Choose the Lasso tool, select the inner and outer edge of the 'Handle' in turn and apply gradient shadows on a slant from both the top and the bottom.

14

Choose the Lasso tool and select an area of the coffee surface to become 'Waves.' Set the foreground color to a slightly lighter shade of brown (R:156, G:117, B:55) and fill the selection.

15

Merge the various cup parts into one layer named 'Large Cup.' Duplicate the 'Large Cup' layer. Reduce the copy to about 20% of the initial size by choosing Edit > Transform > Scale to make a small cup. Rename the 'Large Cup copy' layer to 'Small Cup.'

16

Next, create a new layer named 'Sketch' on which to draw the character. Draw a rough sketch using an appropriate paintbrush, then create new layers beneath it to draw each part of the character separately, including the arms, body and beak. Decide on a position for the small cup created in Step 15 and move the 'Small Cup' layer above the 'Sketch' layer.

17

Create layers in the order of 'Far Arm,' 'Head and Back,' 'Stomach and Face,' 'Beak,' 'Eyes,' 'Glasses' and 'Near Arm.' Set the foreground color to purple (R:128, G:54, B:189). Choose the Lasso or Pencil tool and draw the outline of each part. Fill in each selection with the foreground color. Place a check in the Preserve Transparency check box. Choose the Airbrush tool and add highlights and shadows, periodically changing the brightness and saturation of the foreground color.

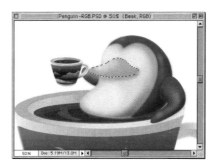

18

For the eyes, choose the Elliptical Marquee tool, hold down the shift (Shift) key and draw the selection for the iris. Fill in the selection with the same color as the body. Select circles on top of the iris to become the pupils. Fill the pupils with black. Set the foreground color to white, choose the Airbrush tool, select a relatively large soft-edged brush and add highlights to the top left to resemble light reflecting from the eyes.

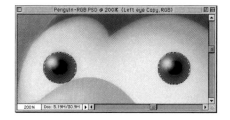

19

Create a layer named 'Glasses.' Set the foreground color to dark purple (R:100, G:11, B:122). Choose the Elliptical Marquee tool and draw the selection that will become the lens frames. Choose Edit > Stroke and set the Width to 6 pixels, Location to Center and Opacity to 100%. Choose the Line or Pencil tool and draw the rest of the frame.

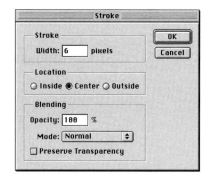

20

Select the lens of the glasses with the Magic Wand tool. Choose Edit > Fill. Set the options to the diagram values and fill in the lens selection. Hide the 'Eyes' layer.

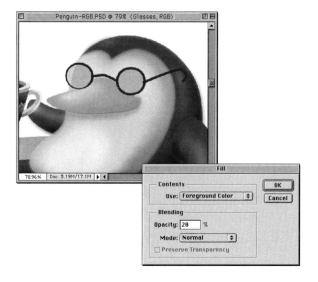

21

We will now make the lenses appear clouded using the general procedure used to create the icebergs earlier. Keep the lens area selected, choose the Polygon Lasso tool, hold down the option (Alt) key and draw a selection of the areas that will not become clouded. Set the foreground color to white. Choose the Linear Gradient tool, set the Gradient option to 'Foreground to Transparent' and apply the gradient. If all the character parts are complete, you may delete the 'Sketch' layer and merge all the parts into one 'Penguin' layer.

22

To make the area where the penguin intersects the liquid look natural, choose the Blur tool and apply it to the bottom portion of the penguin. Make the 'Large Cup' layer active, choose the Magic Wand tool, hold down the shift (Shift) key and click the tool several times on different colored areas of the coffee. Choose the Elliptical Marquee tool, hold down the option (Alt) key and select some areas to snip away parts of the liquid, leaving the impression that the penguin's stomach can be seen through part of the liquid.

23

Copy and paste the selection. Move the newly formed layer above the 'Penguin' layer and reduce the Opacity to about 40%.

24

Now add the finishing touches to the background. First, copy and paste the 'Scenery' file again, and move the resulting layer immediately above the 'Background' layer. Shift the layer slightly higher on the canvas. Add frames to the top and bottom of the picture by creating a new layer and drawing a narrow rectangular selection across the top of the picture. Set the foreground color to beige (R:243, G:207, B:120) and fill in the selection.

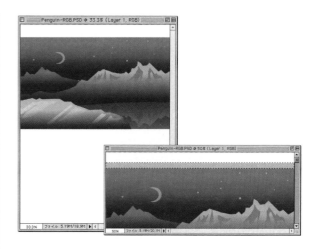

25

Select the top slice of the beige rectangle and set the foreground color to brown (R:208, G:171, B:79). Choose the Linear Gradient tool, set the Gradient option to 'Foreground to Transparent' and drag from the right to about the middle of the picture. Next, select the remaining bottom slice, and apply the gradient from top to bottom. Select, fill and apply gradients to the frame on the bottom of the image using the same procedures. Link and merge this layer to the 'Background' layer.

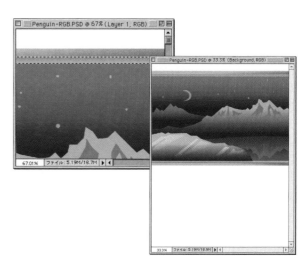

26

Next, choose the Smudge tool and distort the area within the 'Background' layer where steam appears to be rising from the cup. Create a new layer named 'Steam' in which to draw the steam and place it at the very top of the Layers palette. Choose the Airbrush tool and set the Pressure to 10%. Set the foreground color to cream (R:240, G:230, B:188) and draw the steam with a large brush between 45 and 100 pixels in diameter. Change the brightness here and there to give it a soft, billowing look.

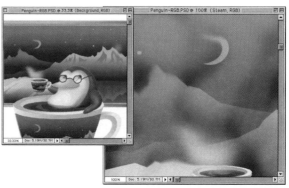

27

Lastly, add a shadow at the bottom of the cup. Create a new layer named 'Shadow' and place it beneath the 'Large Cup' layer. Choose the Elliptical Marquee tool and draw an ellipse slightly larger than the bottom of the cup at its bottom. Hold down the shift (Shift) key and draw another ellipse slightly smaller than the handle that partly overlaps the main shadow.

28

Choose Select > Feather and set the Feather Radius to 5 pixels. Fill the shadow with a light gray (R:201, G:201, B:201) to complete the image.

USING LIGHTING EFFECTS TO FILL OUT CHARACTERS

Try using lighting effects to give characters a softer, fuller look.

1

Create a new file that is approximately 1,800 x 1,800 pixels (15 x 15 cm). Set the Resolution to 300 ppi and the Contents to Transparent. Use a lower resolution if your computer system has limited memory. Choose the Linear Gradient tool and click on the Edit button on the Gradient Tool Options palette to display the Gradient Editor. Choose New and name the result 'Snowy Sky.' Adjust the settings to apply a three-color gradient as shown in the diagram. From the left, set the colors to navy blue (R:0, G:61, B:124), blue-green (R:0, G:149, B:163) and light blue (R:0, G:161, B:189). Click OK.

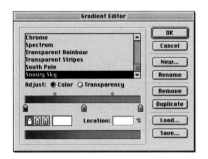

2

Create a new layer. Select about 80% of the canvas with the Rectangular Marquee tool as shown in the diagram and drag the Linear Gradient tool from the top to the bottom to apply the gradient.

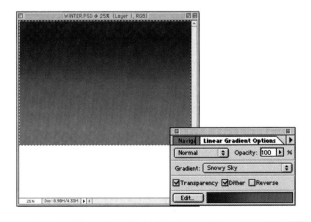

3

Choose Select > Inverse and fill the lower section with a light sky blue (R:5, G:188, B:240). Keep the selection selected and choose Filter > Texture > Craquelure. Set the options to the diagram values to create the appearance of frozen ground.

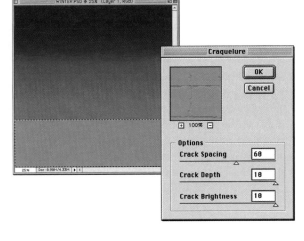

4

To provide the sense of frozen, slippery ground, choose Filter > Render > Lighting Effects and set the options to the diagram values. Set the Texture Channel to Blue and the Height to 100 before applying the effect to the image. Rename 'Layer 1' as 'Background.'

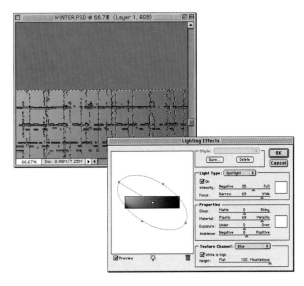

5

Once the background image is close to completion, create a new 'Sketch' layer above the 'Background' layer. Choose the Paintbrush tool and draw a rough sketch of the main character.

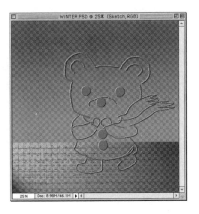

6

Next, use the sketch as a reference to create a path for each part. Wherever the path is difficult to see, reduce the Opacity of the 'Background' layer. Choose the Elliptical Marquee tool and select the outlines, using the sketch below as a reference. Click the Paths palette and click the 'Make work path from selection' icon at the bottom or choose Paths palette menu > Create Work Path to change the selection to a path. Adjust the paths with the Direct-Selection tool and save the paths.

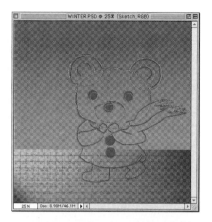

7

Create paths for each part of the character with the same procedures, then copy and paste them to group them all in one path. Where parts overlap, such as the ears and head, create complete, separate paths for both parts, since one outline lies behind the other. The arms too should be divided into upper and lower sections and created separately. After you have created all the paths, delete the 'Sketch' layer. Note that the paths are available on the supplementary CD-ROM by opening Images > 3-06 > 3-06_300.psd or 3-06_150.psd.

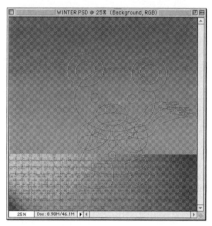

TIPS

Paths are convenient because their colors and shape can be changed, they can be imported into other files and they are easier to use than starting a drawing from scratch. Since the Freeform pen has been included in Photoshop since Version 5.0, even novices unaccustomed to anchor points will find them easy to use. See p39 for instructions on how to use paths.

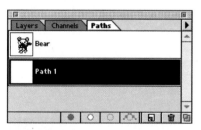

8

Now add the impression of fullness to the paths created in Step 7 while applying colors.Start from the parts that are the farthest in the background and work toward the front, filling each part on a separate layer. Begin by creating a new layer named 'Bear 1.' Choose the Direct Selection tool and select the path for the bear's boots. Set the foreground color to red (R: 225, G: 39, B:51).

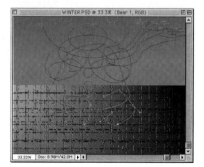

9

Choose Paths palette menu > Make Selection, set the Feather Radius to 4 pixels and click OK.

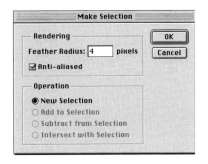

10

Choose Edit > Stroke and set the Width to 4 pixels and the Location to Center to draw a smudged outline. Choose Edit > Fill to color the selection.

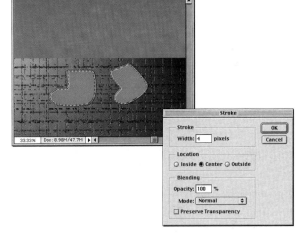

11

Choose Filter > Texture > Grain and set the options to the diagram values. Deselect the selection for just one boot.

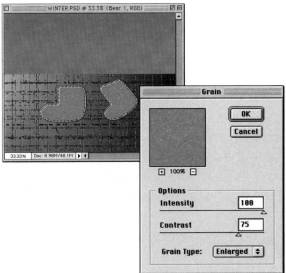

12

Choose Filter > Render > Lighting Effects and set the Texture Channel to Red to give the boot a 3-D shadow. This method provides more depth with a more natural appearance than shadows created with a paintbrush.

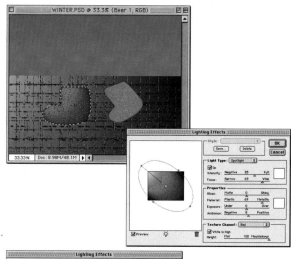

13

Repeat Steps 8 to 12 for each part, working from the farthest to the nearest in the order of 'Boots,' 'Far Scarf,' 'Body,' 'Buttons,' 'Upper Arms,' 'Neck Scarf,' 'Ears,' 'Face,' 'Mouth,' 'Hands,' 'Lower Arms,' 'Eyes' and 'Nose.' Apply only the Lighting Effects filter, setting the Texture channel to None for some selections and changing the settings for other selections depending on the part.

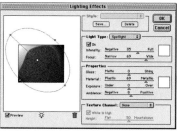

TIPS

If several procedures need to be performed repeatedly, you can increase your efficiency by recording them with the Actions palette. You can then reapply the procedures with the click of a single button. The Actions file for Steps 9 to 12 is available on the supplementary CD-ROM by opening Images > 3-06 > winter.atn. See p37 for instructions on using the Actions palette.

14

Fill the eyes and nose with black. Keep them selected, choose Filter > Render > Lens Flare and set the options to the diagram values to add light.

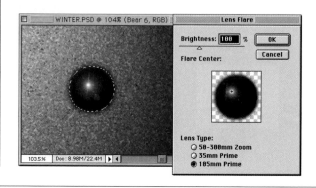

15

Once all the parts have been colored, select each part lacking shadows in turn. Choose a dark foreground color, choose the Paintbrush tool and add shadows. To make the 'Mouth' border stand out particularly well, select a slightly smaller area than the entire mouth and add a dark shadow to the right-hand side. This completes the character portion of the illustration.

16

Now work on the background. Make the 'Background' layer active. Set the foreground color to white, choose the Paintbrush tool and draw snow with a soft-edged brush. Keep changing the size and pressure of the brush as snow is added. Choose Filter > Render > Lens Flare and add highlights to appropriate snowflakes to make the light seem to loom out of the sky.

17

Lastly, create a new layer named 'Shadow' and place it immediately above the 'Background' layer. Set the foreground color to black and the Opacity to 30%. Draw a shadow at the feet of the character to complete your illustration.

BACKGROUNDS FROM CHARACTERS

Try drawing other characters with the procedures used to draw the bear.
Then use these characters as patterns for backgrounds.

1

Sketch other animals, as you did the bear, by combining ellipses created with the Elliptical Marquee tool or created as paths. Create a new file with the Contents set to Transparent and draw a rabbit. Use the bear's path and merely change its ears to create an image that looks like a rabbit.

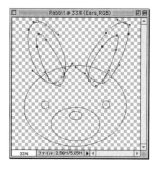

2

Next we'll draw a frog about the same size. Draw one ellipse for the crescent shaped frog's mouth, then hold down the option (Alt) key and draw another slightly above the first and erase the overlapping area of the selection. These paths are saved on the supplementary CD-ROM as Images > 3-06 > Applications > animal_300.psd or animal_150.psd.

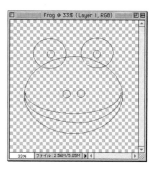

3

As with the bear, create a layer for each part, fill it while blurring the selection and choose Filter > Texture > Grain. A rougher density has been set for the frog in this example than for the rabbit.

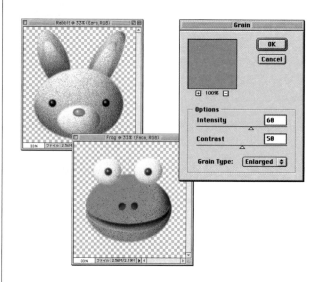

4

Now we'll create a bustling background. First, place both the rabbit and frog onto separate layers, and copy and paste them onto a large canvas as shown. Create a 'Background' layer beneath them, and color each section of the background separately with colors to match each character.

5

Copy the 'Rabbit' layer. Choose Layer > Transform > Scale to scale down the image to the size to be used for the pattern. In this example, we reduced the image to about 20% of its initial size.

6

Select the small rabbit and copy it. Create a new file with the Contents set to Transparent and the same settings as the previous file, then paste the small rabbit selection into it. Choose Select > All and choose Edit > Define Pattern. The small rabbit is now recorded as a pattern.

215

7

Make the initial file active and delete the 'Rabbit Copy' layer. Create a new layer above the 'Background' layer named 'Pattern.' Choose the Rectangular Marquee tool and select the area behind the frog. Choose Edit > Fill, and set the Use option to Pattern. The background of the frog will now be filled with the rabbit pattern.

8

Perform the same procedure on the frog to define it as a pattern. Fill in the background of the rabbit with the frog pattern to complete the illustration.

Chapter ③

BIRTHDAY CARDS

Design unique cards that combine variations of single illustrations that
are enlarged, reduced or reproduced in different colors.

BUSINESS CARDS/SYSTEM NOTEBOOK REFILLS

Show off with your own line of original goods
while adding some fun to products used for business.

NEW YEARS GREETING CARDS

What better way to get your greeting cards noticed than to spice them up with your own flare. Show both your individuality and your talents with computer graphics.

Chapter ③

COFFEE MUGS

You can have your designs printed onto coffee cups by placing an order with your photo developer, output service bureau or Internet-based supplier. These are perfect for commemorative events.

INDEX